The Economics of Digital Markets

Essays in Theoretical and Empirical Industrial Organization

Enrick Arnaud-Joufray

Introduction by Thibaud Vergé
Foreword by Marc Bourreau

Concurrences
2024

Paris – New York – London

106 West 32nd Street, Suite 144 New York, NY, 10001, USA
www.concurrences.com
book@concurrences.com

First Printing, September 2024
978-1-954750-69-2 (Paperback)

Library of Congress Control Number: 2024943888

Cover Design: Yves Buliard, www.yvesbuliard.fr
Book Design and Layout implementation: Nord Compo

Concurrences Books

Tributes

James F. Rill, *P. Lugard, J. Taladay (eds.), Forthcoming 2024*

Eleanor M. Fox – Antitrust Ambassador to the World, *2021*

Herbert Hovenkamp – The Dean of American Antitrust Law, *2021*

Frédéric Jenny – Standing Up for Convergence and Relevance in Antitrust, (Vol. I & II), *2019 & 2021*

Albert Foer – A Consumer Voice in the Antitrust Arena, *2020*

Richard Whish – Taking Competition Law Outside the Box, *2020*

Douglas H. Ginsburg – An Antitrust Professor on the Bench (Vol. I & II), *2018 & 2020*

Wang Xiaoye – The Pioneer of Competition Law in China, *A. Emch, W. Ng (eds.), 2019*

Ian S. Forrester – A Scot without Borders (Vol. I & II), *A. Komninos (eds.), 2015*

William E. Kovacic – An Antitrust Tribute (Vol. I & II), *2013 & 2014*

Practical Books

The DMA and more – Future application and margin of manoeuvre for national jurisdictions, *G. Muscolo & A. Massolo (eds.), Forthcoming 2024*

AI & Competition Policy, *A. Abbott, T. Schrepel (eds.), Forthcoming 2024*

State Aid & National Enforcement, *J. Derenne, D. Jouve, C. Lemaire, F. Martucci (eds.), Forthcoming 2024*

The 2023 U.S. Merger Guidelines: A Review, *S. Sullivan (ed.), 2024*

Competition Inspections in 25 Jurisdictions 2nd Edition – A Practitioner's Guide, *N. Jalabert-Doury (ed.), 2024*

EU Antitrust Enforcement – Law, Economics, History, *Policy & Practice, Wouter P. J. Wils, 2024*

The EU Foreign Subsidies Regulation, *Andreas Reindl, Isabelle Van Damme, 2024*

Compendium of Antitrust Damages Action – International Chamber of Commerce (ICC) – 2nd edition, *J. W.H. Denton AO, F. Brunet, S. Williams, C. Inthavisay (eds.), 2023*

Pharmaceutical Antitrust: An Analysis of US and EU Law, *M. Thill-Tayara, G. Gordon (eds.), 2023*

Innovation Paradox in Merger Control, *G. Gurkaynak, 2023*

Antitrust and the Digital Economy, *Y. Katsoulacos (ed.), 2023 (in collaboration with CRESSE)*

Judicial Review of Competition Cases, *D. Ginsburg, T. Eicke (eds.), 2023*

Competition Law Treatment of Joint Ventures, *B. Bleicher, N. Campbell, A. Hamilton, N. Hukkinen, A. Khan, A. Mordaunt (eds.), 2022 (in collaboration with the IBA)*

Information Exchange & Related Risks, *Z. Marosi, M. Soares (eds.), 2022 (in collaboration with the IBA)*

Rulemaking Authority of the US Federal Trade Commission, *D. Crane (ed.), 2022*

The International Competition Network at Twenty, *D. Anderson & P. Lugard (eds.), 2022*

Competition Case Law Digest – 5th Edition, *F. Jenny, N. Charbit (eds.), 2022*

Competition Inspections in 21 Jurisdictions – A Practitioner's Guide, *N. Jalabert-Doury (ed.), 2022*

Perspectives on Antitrust Compliance, *A. Riley, A. Stephan, A. Tubbs (eds.), 2022 (in collaboration with the ICC)*

Turkish Competition Law, *G. Gürkaynak, 2021*

Competition Law – Climate Change & Environmental Sustainability, *S. Holmes, D. Middelschulte, M. Snoep (eds.), 2021*

Merger Control in Latin America – A Jurisdictional Guide, *P. Burnier da Silveira, P. Sittenfeld (eds.), 2020*

Competition Inspections under EU Law – A Practitioner's Guide, *N. Jalabert-Doury, 2020*

Gun Jumping in Merger Control – A Jurisdictional Guide, *C. Hatton, Y. Comtois, A. Hamilton (eds.), 2019 (in collaboration with the IBA)*

Choice – A New Standard for Competition Analysis? *P. Nihoul (ed.), 2016*

PhD Theses

Abuse of Platform Power, *F. Bostoen, 2023*

Reform of Chinese State-Owned Enterprises, *X. Bai, 2023*

Competition & Regulation in Network Industries – Essays in Industrial Organization, *J-M. Zogheib, 2021*

The Role of Media Pluralism in the Enforcement of EU Competition Law, *K. Bania, 2019*

Buyer Power, *I. Herrera Anchustegui, 2017*

General Interest

Why Competition? Voices from the Antitrust Community and Beyond, *D. Crane, D. Gerard, R. Tritell (eds.), Forthcoming 2024*

Global Dictionary of Competition Law, *D. Healey, W. Kovacic, P. Trevisan, R. Whish (eds.), Forthcoming 2024*

The 5 Labours of Europe, *P.-E. Partsch, 2024*

Great Antitrust Enforcers, *W. E. Kovacic, 2023*

Competition – How to Speak Like an Expert, *E. Combe, 2023*

Women and Antitrust – Voices from the Field (Vol I & II), *E. Kurgonaite & K. Nordlander, 2020*

e-Book versions available for **Concurrences+** subscribers

DISCLAIMER

This book is based on my doctoral thesis defended in December 2022 at the Institut Polytechnique de Paris (Telecom Paris) before a jury composed of Professor Bruno Jullien (CNRS and Toulouse School of Economics), Professor Wilfried Sand-Zantman (ESSEC Business School), Professor Christine Zulehner (University of Vienna), Professor José-Luis Moraga- Gonzàles (Vrije Universiteit Amsterdam), Mr. François Jeanjean (Research Engineer, Orange) and Professor Marc Bourreau, (Telecom Paris). The thesis was supervised by Professor Marc Bourreau, who did me the honor of writing the preface of the book. I am also grateful to the members of the jury for writing their testimonials to the book.

The book has been slightly modified so that its "scientific apparatus" is as up-to-date as possible. Still, some of the work presented here is still under progress, and any error that may appear is the author's sole responsibility.

The author declares that there is no conflict of interest associated with this publication. The opinions expressed in this book are those of the author. Telecom Paris (Institut Polytechnique de Paris) neither approves nor disapproves of them. The book won the Concurrences PhD Award in Economics 2023, chaired by Professor Thibaud Vergé (French Competition Authority), Professor Claire Chambolle (INRAE), Griet Jans (Belgian Competition Authority), and Alexis Walckiers (E.CA Economics).

TABLE OF CONTENTS

ACKNOWLEDGEMENTS

First and foremost, I would like to express my deepest gratitude to my supervisor, Marc Bourreau. When I was a student at ENSAE in 2018, I was looking for a master thesis advisor in the field of digital economics. All the recommendations I received then pointed toward one direction: Marc Bourreau. Marc kindly accepted to supervise my work while barely knowing me. This experience went so well that when I decided to pursue a PhD months later, I could not think of anyone else to supervise my thesis. Marc guided me through the construction of an economic model, a much different task than understanding the theory. He provided invaluable advice throughout my PhD, read several versions of the work presented in this manuscript, and suggested many corrections. I cannot thank him enough for his support throughout this journey.

This endeavour would not have been possible without the support of Orange, which funded this thesis during several years. I want to thank Marc Lebourges for his faith and continuous support to economic research, and François Jeanjean, for his encouragements, kindness and many useful advices throughout the years. I also thank colleagues at Orange for many interesting discussions: Julienne, Louise, Jean-Baptiste, Lionel, Stéphane, Anne-Marie, Volcy, Marie-Noémie, Pauline, Louisa and Thierry.

Words cannot express my gratitude to the members of the jury, who accepted to devote some of their precious time to evaluate my work. Much of the work presented in this thesis was influenced by the extensive contributions of these authors. I am extremely grateful to Bruno Jullien for accepting to be the president of this jury. I had the privilege to benefit from his insights in competition policy when I was a student in the Master of Economics and Competition Law at TSE; and from his invaluable advice later on, as part of the partnership program between Orange and TSE. I would like to express my deepest appreciation to Wilfried Sand-Zantman and Christine Zulehner, who accepted to be the referees of this thesis. Wilfried introduced me to the theory of industrial organization when I was just a bachelor student at TSE. His teaching has been very inspiring and largely influenced my current research interests. I was lucky to benefit from his advice over the last years, and I look forward to interacting with him in the next future at ESSEC business school. Christine has been a very important member of the research environment at Telecom Paris for several years. She has been very supportive of Ph.D. students, engaging in several fruitful collaborations with them. I regret that the pandemic deprived me from the opportunity to interact with her as much as I would have wanted to. I am extremely grateful to José-Luis Moraga-Gonzáles, who also accepted to be part of this jury. I met José-Luis a few months ago at Télécom Paris, although I was already familiar with some of his many contributions to the economic literature. He was very generous with his time and provided me with many comments on the first chapter of this thesis.

I would like to extend my profound gratitude to Yassine Lefouili. I met Yassine when I was a master student at TSE. His dedication to the master program and his inspiring teaching were determinant in my decision to pursue a Ph.D. My debt to Yassine extends well beyond my studies at TSE. He wrote a recommendation letter that allowed me to enter ENSAE. He was part of my Ph.D. midterm committee. He made several detailed comments and suggestions on each of the three chapters of this thesis. I am very indebted to him for all his support throughout these years.

I am thankful for the exciting environments I benefited from at TSE, ENSAE and Telecom Paris over the last decade. I was particularly lucky to witness the attribution of the 2014 Nobel Prize in Economics to Jean Tirole, and to attend the special lectures he gave to students of the school the next year. Many thanks to the faculty members of each of these institutions, and more particularly to Doh-Shin Jeon, Alexandre de Cornière, Thibaud Vergé, Marie-Laure Allain, Roxana Fernandez, Michelangelo Rossi, Lukasz Grzybowski, Ulrich Laitenberger, Laurie Ciaramella and Grazia Cecere (from IMT Business School).

I would like to thank all the Ph.D. students and Post-doc researchers I had the opportunity to interact with. Ángela Muñoz and Vicente Lagos gave me a warm welcome in their office when I started my Ph.D. I was particularly lucky to start a collaboration with Vicente and benefit from his experience. I had the pleasure to spend most of my Ph.D. time with Adrien Raizonville. His devotion and enthusiasm to improve public policies are inspiring. We have become close friends, and I thank him very much for his continuous support. I also thank Guillaume Thébaudin, Pierre-François Darlas, Chiara Belletti, Jean-Marc Zogheib, Arrah-Marie Jo, Ambre Nicolle and Alexis Larousse. Many thanks to Julien Monardo and Hugo Molina, with whom I had many discussions on empirical industrial organization, and who gave me many tips for the job market.

I am grateful to Xavier Lambin, who gave me his trust to start a new exciting project with him at ESSEC Business School. I cannot wait to join ESSEC's department after the completion of my Ph.D.

Many thanks to my friends for their razor-sharp sense of humour and all the good times we spent together over the last ten years, in particular to Vincent, Salim, Théo, Marouane, Thomas and Smaïl.

I could not have undertaken this journey without the support of my family. My parents, Anne and Patrick, instilled me with values that allowed me to go through this demanding journey. They developed my understanding of the world and helped me observe how people behave, one of the most important prerequisite in economic research. They taught me respect, open-mindedness, humour, and humility. My brother, Loïc, my sister, Marine and my brother-in-law, Aurélien, shared both positive and more difficult moments with me and provided useful advice at key moments. I also thank my in-laws, with whom I spent many cheerful moments. I feel privileged to be surrounded by such wonderful people.

Finally, I would like to thank my wife, Nacera, for her endless support and encouragement over the last nine years. She listened to me talking about my different projects for hours without falling asleep (well, almost). She provided me with many advices and suggestions. She cheered me up in difficult times. Thank you for sharing my life, and carrying our baby. Over the last few months, he represented the greatest motivation for finishing my thesis on time.

INTRODUCTION

In June 2023, as president of the jury for the Concurrences Economics Ph.D. Award, I had the great pleasure of awarding this prize to Enrick Arnaud-Joufray, for several reasons. Firstly, and although this had nothing to do with the jury's decision, because I have been able to see Enrick's progress over the last few years. He was one of my students in industrial economics, in the Master in Economics at Institut Polytechnique de Paris, and following several discussions about his thesis topic, I suggested that he get in touch with my colleague Marc Bourreau. The latter subsequently agreed to supervise Enrick's PhD thesis, which Enrick undertook within the Télécom Paris and Orange teams.

Secondly, and above all, because of the high quality of his work. The jury for this thesis award – which included Claire Chambolle (Director of Research at INRAe Paris-Saclay), Grief Jans (Chief Economist at the Belgian Competition Authority) and Alexis Walckiers (Director at E.CA Economics) – particularly appreciated the variety of methodological tools used in this thesis. Indeed, while the first two chapters are essentially theoretical, i.e. based on the construction and resolution of formalized models of industrial economics, the third chapter consists of the econometric estimation of a structural model. Furthermore, the subjects covered by the three chapters, at the frontier between the economics of competition and regulation, using the tools of industrial economics and the economics of networks and platforms, demonstrate the wide range of instruments available to Enrick.

Although I will not describe Enrick's work in detail, for which my eminent colleague Marc Bourreau who followed Enrick during his thesis years is much better qualified in any case, I would like to emphasize the importance of the contributions made by this work.

The first chapter of this thesis is devoted to analyzing the competition of digital platforms whose business model is based on advertising. Competition for advertising revenues tends to reduce differentiation between platforms: by differentiating itself from its competitor, a platform will tend to attract 'multi-platform' consumers – who therefore seek different services on different platforms – consumers who are less 'remunerative' insofar as advertisers can reach them through each of the platforms. One of the important implications of this model concerns merger control: a merger between platforms can lead to greater differentiation – due to a strategic repositioning of the platforms post-merger – which can benefit consumers but will lead to higher prices for advertisers.

The second chapter focuses less on competition issues and more on platform regulation. Enrick examines the transparency and quality of reviews provided by a platform. Unsurprisingly, more regulation of reviews (in terms of content, for example) benefits consumers.

Finally, the last chapter studies the impact of the entry of a new operator on the mobile telephony market in Chile. As this operator did not develop its own network but used its access to the network of one of its competitors, the impact of entry was not identical on the three pre-existing competitors. In fact, the operator providing access had less incentive to react aggressively to the entry of the new operator than its competitors: even if its market share – and therefore its profitability – on the retail market was negatively affected by entry, this was offset for it (but not for its competitors) by the revenues generated on the upstream market. Based on the econometric estimation of a structural model allowing the simulation of counterfactual situations, Enrick was able to explore how the situation would have been affected by the identity of the operator providing access to the new entrant. Once again, this chapter is particularly relevant for both regulators and merger control, as it shows how the tools of structural econometrics can be used to better select remedies (structural or behavioral, such as an obligation to provide access).

Following his thesis, Enrick has chosen to pursue an academic career and I hope that he will soon be able to publish his work in the best scientific journals and continue to offer us work of this quality.

Thibaud Vergé
Vice President, French Competition Authority

FOREWORD

It is with great pleasure that I write this preface for Enrick Arnaud-Joufray's book, based on his doctoral thesis which I had the pleasure of supervising at Télécom Paris. This work is the culmination of a remarkable doctoral career, which saw Enrick Arnaud-Joufray develop original research in industrial economics, with important implications for sectoral regulation and competition policy.

Mr. Arnaud-Joufray's research focuses on competition and regulation in network industries. Network industries are characterised by strong economies of scale in production and significant network effects in consumption. The increasing returns favour the emergence of dominant players. In the digital sector, several platforms have become key players. They rely on specific, multi-sided business models, with advertising as their main source of revenue. They exploit massive data collected from their users that can be used to improve the recommendation tools that guide consumers in their choice of products or services. In the telecommunications sector, the same trend towards concentration is undergoing. Sectoral regulators must then resort to specific measures, such as access obligations, to allow the entry and development of new players. Enrick Arnaud-Joufray's work seeks to shed light on the relationship between the structure of these markets, the strategies of the players and public policy.

Mr Arnaud-Joufray's research draws on a variety of methodological tools from industrial economics, network economics and platform economics to showcase highly topical issues in the digital and telecommunications sectors.

Mr Arnaud-Joufray's thesis is composed of three distinct chapters, each organised around a specific research question.

In the first chapter, Mr. Arnaud-Joufray examines the incentives to differentiate for platforms that are free to users and financed by advertising. Each platform offers consumers a service with various functionalities. Platforms are differentiated when the features they offer don't overlap perfectly. When this happens, some consumers see an interest in joining both platforms, while other consumers decide to only use one platform. Differentiation therefore affects the composition of the demand that each platform seeks to monetise from advertisers. Insofar as exclusive users are more valuable on the advertising market than users who are also present on the competing platform(s), a platform has relatively little incentive to differentiate, as this will reduce the value of its audience by changing its composition. Enrick Arnaud-Joufray shows that differentiation at market equilibrium is less when platforms are financed by advertising, than when they are financed directly by users.

The second chapter looks at a situation where an agent can rely on the advice of an expert before taking a decision. One problem for the agent is that the expert may be biased; he may have a personal interest in guiding the agent towards a decision that is favourable to him. In particular, the expert may only reveal information that encourages the agent to make a decision that benefits him. In this context, Enrick Arnaud-Joufray studies whether a regulation requiring the expert to disclose a minimum amount of information could be beneficial for the agent. For example, the platforms that publish restaurant reviews, such as TripAdvisor or Google, could impose a minimum length for these reviews. Mr. Arnaud-Joufray shows that this type of regulation is not always effective. However, when the regulator can influence the effort made by the expert to provide relevant advice, a minimum quota of information is always desirable.

The third and final chapter looks at the Chilean mobile telecommunications market. In 2015, a fourth operator, WOM, entered the market. The arrival of this new competitor led to a fall in prices and reduced the market shares of the incumbent operators. However, the three incumbent operators were not affected in the same way by WOM's entry. Entel, the operator that provided access to its network to the new entrant, reduced its retail prices less in response to entry than the other incumbents and suffered a greater loss of market share. According to Enrick Arnaud-Joufray and his co-author Vicente Lagos, the economic mechanism at work is that Entel's incentives to defend its market share on the retail market were reduced by the revenues made by providing access to WOM. They demonstrate this rigorously by developing a structural model to simulate counterfactual situations, such as having a different operator, other than Entel, provide WOM with access to its network.

This innovative research, both theoretical and empirical, sheds light on the network and digital industries, while also offering relevant insights for public policy in these markets.

The first chapter shows that a merger between platforms financed by advertising can increase the differentiation of services to the benefit of consumers while increasing prices for advertisers. This suggests that a competition authority should consider the incentives to reposition products after the merger.

The second chapter shows that regulating the recommendations and reviews submitted by platforms can benefit consumers by reducing possible biases.

Finally, the third chapter shows that the entry of a new mobile operator affects the behaviour of incumbent operators differently depending on whether they provide access to their network to the new entrant or not. For a sectoral regulator who must accompany the entry of a new player, the identity of the operator providing access is therefore not neutral.

The high quality of this thesis earned it the Concurrences Award, granted by eminent specialists in both competition law and economics. The three different chapters making up the thesis have also been presented at several other prestigious conferences, and are destined to be published in peer-reviewed scientific journals in economics.

I wish Mr. Arnaud-Joufray every success in the pursuit of his professional career.

Marc Bourreau
Professor, Télécom Paris, Institut Polytechnique de Paris

INTRODUCTION

1. The field of microeconomics is concerned with the way individuals and firms make decisions, and how these decisions translate into aggregate outcomes. Economic agents typically respond to different incentives, as is illustrated by economist Stephen Landsburg's famous quote: "Economics can be summed up in four words: people respond to incentives. The rest is commentary." A critical issue is to determine how we can organize the economy so as to cater to the needs and objectives of these different agents. While the market economy has proven successful to achieve economic well-being, it can also be a source of market failures. Industrial organization identifies market power as a prominent cause of market failure and studies the conditions under which market power is more likely to arise. A general tenet in industrial organization is that market structure is closely related to market power, and that competition leads to more efficient economic outcomes. However, several markets exhibit particular characteristics that make competition difficult to sustain.

2. A natural example is offered by the telecommunication industry. This market is characterized by high fixed costs and thus large economies of scale. These factors favor concentration and make entry difficult. Market concentration may lead to high prices, depriving some consumers of access to an essential service. The importance of access to telecommunications services is exemplified by the recent COVID-19 pandemic, where billions of people relied on them to work and communicate. A recent OECD report reveals that internet traffic increased by 60% shortly after the emergence of the pandemic.[1] Studying the factors that can facilitate entry and increase competition in telecommunications markets is thus of primary importance.[2]

3. The development of digital markets also raises new challenges for public policy.[3] These markets exhibit significant economies of scale and network externalities,

1 OECD, *Keeping the Internet Up and Running in Times of Crisis*, 2020. See also, OECD, Digital Economy Outlook Supplement, *Digital Transformation in the Age of Covid-19*, 2020.

2 For empirical studies assessing the effects of entry in telecommunications market, see Nicolle, Grzybowski and Zulehner (2018), Bourreau, Sun and Verboven (2021), and Seim and Viard (2011).

3 See Tirole (2016) for a thorough discussion of the challenges faced by the digital economy.

which has led to the emergence of powerful companies over the last decades. Competition authorities want to understand better how these platforms work and need to adapt their tools to analyze these markets. The recent reports by Crémer, de Montjoye and Schweitzer (2019), Furman (2019), and Stigler (2019), among others, illustrate the important policy discussions surrounding platforms. Indeed, while platforms provide consumers with valuable and often free services, their business model often relies on advertising to derive revenues. This feature may significantly affect the strategic decisions of these firms, in particular as regards to the collection and use of consumer data. In a recent survey, 70% of US business leaders declared that their company increased collection of consumer personal data over the last year.[4] In the same survey, 86% of US citizens said that data privacy is a growing concern for them. In Europe, the General Regulation for Data Protection came into effect on May 25, 2018 and gives consumer more control over the use of their data. As we shall see, product differentiation is another strategic dimension that may be affected by a platform's business model.

4. Many digital platforms provide rich information to consumers, which help them make better informed decisions when choosing an hotel, picking a restaurant or selecting a movie. However, a critical question is to what extent one can rely on platforms' advice, which can potentially be biased. There is ample evidence of businesses manipulating reviews to influence consumers' purchasing decisions.[5] It is thus essential to study how we can make the informational environment more reliable.

5. In this thesis, we study two important issues related to the digital economy. We first analyze firms' incentives to produce differentiated services in advertising-funded markets, how these incentives differ from more traditional markets, and how mergers affect those incentives. Second, we study whether more demanding disclosure policies with respect to online recommendations can help individual decision makers make better informed decisions. These studies form the two first chapters of the thesis. In Section 1 of this introduction, we discuss why it is important to understand how digital platforms work and some of the main issues surrounding them.

6. The third chapter of this thesis is devoted to the analysis of mobile telecommunications markets. We study empirically how providing access to an entrant affects an incumbent pricing strategy in the retail market. We also discuss how patterns of competition in the retail market shape competition in the input market. In Section 2 of the introduction, we discuss regulation and competition policy in telecommunication markets.

---

4 The survey was conducted in 2021 by KPMG. https://info.kpmg.us/news-perspectives/industry-insights-research/data-privacy-survey-orson-lucas.html

5 See: https://www.nytimes.com/2019/11/28/business/online-reviews-fake.html

1.1 The challenges of the digital economy

7. Many of the biggest companies in the world operate in digital markets. As of August 2022, Apple, Alphabet (Google), Amazon, Microsoft, Meta (Facebook) were five of the ten largest market capitalization.[6] Many of the most valuable start-ups are also platform businesses, e.g., Airbnb, BlaBlaCar, Spotify, Uber or Lyft. Digital markets present particular features that differ from more traditional markets. Understanding these peculiarities is essential to properly address the specific issues raised by the digital economy.[7] Competition authorities should thus account for these differences when assessing particular conducts or analyzing the potential effects of a merger.

8. **Characteristics of platforms.** Platforms are firms that operate in multisided markets, i.e., markets in which several different groups of users interact. According to Evans (2003), the existence of a multisided market requires three main conditions. First, there must be two or more groups of users. Second, the interactions between these different groups of users generate externalities, positive or negative. Last, and perhaps most importantly, there must be an intermediary which internalizes the externalities exerted by the different groups of users. A platform is thus a firm that connects different groups of users in a way that generates value.[8]

9. This value could not be generated without the platform. For instance, BlaBlaCar, Uber and Lyft connect drivers with people who are looking for a ride. Drivers and riders exert positive externalities on each other. Indeed, an increase in the number of drivers makes the platform more attractive for riders, as it becomes easier to find a ride (the waiting time decreases in the number of drivers). Similarly, an increase in the number of riders makes the platform more attractive to drivers, since a higher demand increases the potential profits. The presence of such positive cross-group externalities, also called indirect network effects, creates a virtuous circle which, ultimately, leads to an increase in market concentration. This also implies that a monopoly can constitute an efficient market structure.[9] It is very valuable for consumers to be able to access all hotel offers on Booking, and vice versa for hotels. One of the first papers to provide a formal analysis of these indirect network effects is Rochet and Tirole (2003). This paper started circulating in 2000 and paved the way to numerous influential papers studying the economics of platforms (e.g., Caillaud and Jullien, 2003; Armstrong, 2006). However, several markets involving such effects existed long before: newspapers, stock markets, nightclubs, payment cards, etc. The rapid development of the

6 See: https://www.statista.com/statistics/263264/top-companies-in-the-world-by-market-capitalization/

7 For a comprehensive, formal and recent exposition of the economics of platforms, see Belleflamme and Peitz (2021). For a non-technical introduction to the economics of platforms, see Evans and Schmalensee (2016).

8 For a typology of the different types of platforms, see Filistrucchi (2008).

9 Galeotti and Moraga-Gonzáles (2009) show that a monopoly platform does not introduce further distortions than those induced by the market power of the differentiated product sellers (i.e., the seller side of the market).

internet and then mobile networks fostered interactions between individuals and provided platforms with access to data, allowing them to match users efficiently. In some context, the cross-group externalities exerted can be negative. This is, for instance, the case for newspapers and media markets more generally, in which the presence of advertisers upsets readers (Anderson and Coate, 2005). This means that in this type of markets, platforms must carefully control the amount of advertising to avoid losing viewers. This also suggests that competition may be easier to sustain in these environments.

10. **Platform's pricing strategy.** A key challenge for a platform is to reach a critical mass of users. Platforms are not selling products but interactions.[10] Hence, they need a sufficient number of users from the different sides of the market to initiate network effects and grow. Caillaud and Jullien (2003) call this the "Chicken and Egg" problem. Uber cannot attract consumers without a sufficient number of drivers; and drivers do not have any incentives to join Uber if the number of consumers using the platform is too low.

11. The price (or user access fee) constitutes the main strategic variable at the disposal of the platform to attract the different groups of users. According to Rochet and Tirole (2006), the volume of transactions on the platform do not depend solely on the level of prices, but also on the structure of prices. An optimal pricing strategy must account for the cross-group externalities that each group of users exerts on the other. Accounting for cross-group externalities can result in a price below marginal cost and this type of strategy can be profitable even from a dynamic (long run) perspective. The idea is to subsidize one side of the market and extract profits from the other side. Jullien (2011) call such strategies "divide and conquer". This implies that a price lower than marginal cost shall not necessarily be seen as predatory pricing, in contrast to more traditional markets. In general, the group that exerts the strongest cross-group externalities on the other side is the one who is charged the lowest price. In many cases, this group of users is not even charged anything: Google search is free for consumers, dating websites often do not charge women with any fee, social networks such as Facebook or TikTok are free for consumers, and newspapers and TV channels can also often be accessed by readers/viewers without paying. The fact that many platforms rely mostly on advertising to derive revenues has important implications on several other strategic choices. The amount of consumer data collected and sold is an obvious example. In Chapter 1, we show that firms' incentives to produce differentiated services in advertising-financed markets greatly differ from those in more traditional markets.

12. **Competition.** As discussed above, digital markets are characterized by substantial network effects and very low or even zero prices for consumers.

---

10 There are some exceptions. For instance, Amazon acts both as a intermediary and a seller on its own platform. This is also the case for Apple, which operates the App store and develops in-house applications.

These features make it very difficult for an entrant to challenge an incumbent platform.[11] Despite the strength of network effects, we observe situations of sustainable competition between firms.[12] One key element that allows competition between platforms is differentiation. Some markets do not leave much room for differentiation, e.g., search engine or ride-sharing platforms. In other markets, platforms can target different consumer segments, e.g., newspapers (right-wing vs left-wing), dating websites (Tinder vs Meetic), or social networks (TikTok for younger consumers). They can also propose slightly different services to the same broad group of consumers, e.g., social networks (Facebook/Instagram/ Snapchat) or messaging apps (WhatsApp vs Signal/Telegram, which provide different levels of privacy protection). Differentiation can stem from exclusivity, e.g., some video games are only available on some game consoles (Nintendo). However, exclusivity can also lead to market monopolization and competition authorities tend to be very careful with exclusive contracts. When the product sold is rather homogeneous, platforms can differentiate by adopting different business models (Calvano and Polo, 2020), e.g., music streaming services (e.g., Spotify vs Apple Music); TV (ad-financed vs subscription-based). The other key element that allows multiple platforms to coexist is multihoming. Multihoming refers to the idea that consumers can patronize several platforms. It is very frequent in markets where the service is free for consumers, such as online newspapers or social networks. In Chapter 1, we show that multihoming has important implications on firms' incentives to produce differentiated services.

13. **Main current issues.** Despite the important innovations brought by platforms, their economic and social influence raise many issues. We now briefly discuss some of these issues. Perhaps the most debated one relates to data. Data constitute a substantial strategic advantage for platforms. It enables them to propose more relevant content/products to consumers. As we have seen above, data is at the core of several platforms' business model. However, collecting data raises an issue of transparency with respect to consumers. Economists have studied various important issues related to data[13], such as the link between data and price discrimination (Belleflamme and Vergote, 2016; Montes, Sand-Zantman and Valletti, 2018), firm's incentives to preserve consumers' privacy (Jullien, Lefouili and Riordian, 2021), the impact of a cap on data collection on quality investment (Lefouili and Toh, 2022), and the impact of data collection taxation on overall taxation revenues (Bourreau, Caillaud and De Nijs, 2018). The General Data Protection Regulation came into effect in 2018 and introduces more protection regarding the collection and use of consumer data.

---

11 Halaburda, Jullien and Yehezkel (2020) and Biglaiser, Crémer and Veiga (2022) study conditions in which an entrant can challenge an incumbent platform from a dynamic perspective.

12 For a comprehensive review of the literature on platform competition, see Jullien and Sand-Zantman (2021).

13 For a exhaustive and recent literature review on the economics of privacy, see Acquisti (2016).

14. The practice of tying has also been extensively studied by economists over the last decades. A firm with substantial market power in a market tries to conquer another more competitive market. To do so, she ties its dominant product with its other product in the competitive market. The Chicago critique has argued that such a strategy is not profitable for the firm, as she would have to sacrifice too much revenues in the dominant market to conquer the more competitive market. This theory has been recently revisited in multisided markets, and Choi and Jeon (2020) have shown that such a strategy can actually be profitable. This work sheds light on the recent Google Shopping, Android and AdSense cases, for which Google has been fined more than 8 billion euros by the European Commission for abuse of dominant position. On March and April 2022, the European Union adopted two regulations, the Digital Markets Act (DMA) and the Digital Services Act (DSA). The aim of these regulations is to impose greater responsibility to powerful digital platforms, to establish a level playing field and foster competition in the European Union. These regulations identify practices that harm competition and are strongly discouraged (or even prohibited), among which the practice of tying by big platforms.

15. One of the areas not addressed by the aforementioned regulations is merger policy.[14] Merger control must also be adapted in multisided markets.[15] One of the commonly used tools in merger analysis is the Upward Pricing Pressure test. The idea is to estimate the share of a firm's demand that would go to the other merging firm in the event that this firm increases its price. If a substantial part of the lost demand goes to the other merging firm, an increase in prices is to be expected. In two-sided markets, we must account for the fact that a change of demand on one side also affects demand on the other side of the market (Affeldt et al., 2013). The presence of indirect network effects and the stucture of prices make the analysis more ambiguous than in standard markets. The magnitude of search frictions must also be accounted for when assessing the effects of a merger. Moraga-Gonzáles and Petrikaité (2013) show that in markets with substantial search costs, mergers can benefit consumers by allowing for more efficient search. This economic mechanism applies very well to digital markets, in which the number of available products is considerable and platforms allow to reduce search costs. The extent of multihoming behavior also plays an important role in merger analysis in digital markets. In Chapter 1, we contribute to the literature on mergers. We show that consumer multihoming may limit platforms' incentives to differentiate, and that mergers can restore those incentives.

16. Digital platforms provide rich information environments that help us make better informed decisions. These platforms are organizing user recommendations for various products. As underlined by Che and Horner (2018), nowadays, there

14 Although big platforms will have to provide notice of all their acquisitions, the DMA and DSA provide no additional powers to investigate transactions that do not meet the current threshold for intervention.

15 For an empirical analysis of the effects of mergers in more standard markets and in various countries, see Gugler, Mueller, Burcin Yurtoglu, and Zulehner (2002).

is a recommender system for almost any experience good: Yelp for restaurants, TripAdvisor for hotels, IMDb and Rotten Tomatoes for movies. Individuals also use social networks such as Facebook and Twitter to share their opinions and sometimes try to influence people's choices, notably in politics. However, one question that is increasingly debated is how reliable the information provided on digital platforms really is. Fake news has become a widespread phenomenon on platforms and can have detrimental effects on individuals and society. For instance, several studies have shown that fake news is particularly prevalent around election dates.[16] There is also evidence that people sharing their opinions on social media can lead to more political polarization in the society.[17] Some reports have called for a sharp increase in the number of human moderators at social network companies to scrutinize the messages posted.[18] In practice, it is very difficult for platforms to keep all the information generated in check. Indeed, there are millions of opinions, reviews and recommendations posted every day on the internet. One milder form of misinformation than fake news is that people sharing opinions or reviews may sometimes reveal only partial information that is supportive of their views. In some situations, one potential way to make these reviews more informative may be to require more information disclosure. The Federal Trade Commission recently issued some guidelines to make online reviews more reliable.[19] In particular, the FTC notes that "some online retailers and review platforms allow only narrative reviews, or only narrative reviews of a certain minimum length", suggesting that such disclosure policies can potentially make reviews more informative. While digital markets offer a stark illustration, we note that these informational issues are hardly limited to the digital environment. In Chapter 2, we explore the merit of stricter disclosure rules, or minimum message length policy, in environments that involve an informed adviser and an uninformed decision maker.

1.2 Entry and competition in telecommunications markets

17. The telecommunications industry constitutes one of the building block of modern societies. It connects people and allows them to share information at an

16 For a short introduction to the issues related to fake news and some useful references, see Lazer et al. (2018), "The science of fake news".

17 See Bail et al., (2018). Allcott, Braghieri, Eichmeyer and Gentzkow (2020) also show that deactivating Facebook reduces political polarization.

18 See Barrett, Hendrix and Sims (2021), "Fueling the Fire: How Social Media Intensifies U.S. Political Polarization — And What Can Be Done About It.", available at https://bhr.stern.nyu.edu/polarization-report-page.

19 Featuring Online Customer Reviews: A Guide for Platforms. See the FTC's website for more information: https://www.ftc.gov/business-guidance/advertising-marketing/endorsements-influencers-reviews.

unprecedented speed. It has been shown to contribute significantly to countries' growth (Czernich et al., 2011). Making these services accessible to the greatest number of citizens represents a key challenge for policy makers. In developing countries notably, the development of telecommunication networks constitutes a critical issue for the economy. The telecommunications industry also presents characteristics that warrant specific attention by public authorities.

18. The telecommunications industry is characterized by significant network effects, although of a slightly different nature than those described in the previous section.[20] Here, we call such externalities direct network effects, because there is typically one group of users, i.e., consumers. These consumers enjoy interactions with one another and thus, the larger the number of consumers using the network, the higher the value of the overall network. After the invention of the telephone in 1876, telephone companies tried to convince households to subscribe to this new communication service. The idea is that if the service reaches a critical mass of users, it becomes extremely attractive for other users to join.[21] Another salient characteristic of the telecommunications industry is the huge costs required to roll out a network. Such costs imply that network duplication is not always efficient from an economic perspective. This argument has long been one of the main justification behind the existence of state-owned (natural) monopolies. However, a new approach to the supply of telecommunications services was developed in the 1980's and 1990's in the US and in Europe. It was decided to open the telecommunications markets to competition.

19. Historically, two main types of competition for the telecommunications markets have been considered and extensively discussed in the economic literature: "infrastructure competition" and "service competition".[22] Service-based competition was introduced in the 1990's at the moment of liberalization and requires the incumbent to provide access to its infrastructure to new entrants. In Europe, unbundled access of the local loop became mandatory in December 2000 with the regulation No 2887/2000 of the European Parliament and the Council. This regulation allows competition in the broadband retail market, which should benefit consumers in the short term. The ladder of investment hypothesis (Cave, 2006) predicts that, once the entrant earns sufficient profits or market shares and acquires some knowledge about the functioning of the market, it will have incentives to develop its own infrastructure.[23] This should ensure effective competition in the long-run. Regulatory authorities thus organized this progressive transition from service-based to infrastructure-based

---

20 Belleflamme and Peitz (2015) analyze formally the link between direct and indirect network effects.

21 The success of Facebook also relies on such direct network effects. Facebook still constitutes a multisided business as it also allows advertisers to interact with consumers.

22 For comprehensive treatments of the regulatory framework in telecommunications, see Laffont and Tirole (2001) and Bourreau (2016).

23 See Bacache, Bourreau and Gaudin (2014) for an empirical analysis of the ladder of investment

competition. However, this does not mean that firms should ultimately rely exclusively on their own infrastructure. A large part of recent regulation is devoted to the analysis of infrastructure sharing agreements between firms to accelerate the transition to new technologies, and the impact of such agreements on investment and competition.

20. Mobile telecommunications share many characteristics with the aforementioned fixed networks. In particular, the cost to roll out a mobile network is extremely high. In addition, such networks rely on spectrum licenses, which constitute a scarce resource auctioned periodically and at a high price. The entry of new mobile operators often relies on national roaming agreements, which allow new entrants to provide an immediate full geographic coverage to consumers while progressively rolling-out their own network.[24] In some countries, such agreements are imposed by national regulation agencies to facilitate entry and stimulate competition in the market. In other instances, national roaming agreements can be implemented for commercial purposes without the request from the NRA.[25] In this context, it is important to understand what drives incumbent firms' incentives to provide access and the effect of such contracts on competition.[26,27] In Chapter 3, we discuss such incentives and we study empirically how providing access to the entrant affects an incumbent pricing strategy in the retail market.

1.3 Thesis contributions and outline

21. The aim of this thesis is to provide a contribution to some of the issues discussed in this introduction.

22. In Chapter 1, we study how firms' incentives to produce differentiated products in multisided media markets differ from more traditional markets. Consumers' purchasing behavior is shown to play an important role in driving those incentives. We note that in many product markets, some consumers frequently purchase several competing products such as cars, magazines, or various

24 International roaming is perhaps the most well known type of roaming, and allows consumers to use their mobile devices when abroad. In contrast, national roaming refers to the use of networks of operators within the same country.

25 For example, in France, 2G national roaming is enforced by the regulator, while 3G agreements are based on commercial arrangements between operators. For an overview of national roaming regulations in many countries, see the National Roaming for Resilience report by the European Union Agency for Network and Information Security.

26 Ordover and Shaffer (2007) and Bourreau et al. (2011) analyze of the link between access provision and downstream competition. For a discussion of issues related to vertical foreclosure, see Rey and Tirole (2007).

27 It is important to note that more competition need not always be desirable. Jeanjean and Houngbonon (2017) study the link between market structure and investment in mobile telecommunications markets and show that more competition may negatively affect investments.

electronic devices while others stick to one product. In the digital economy, such multipurchasing (or "multihoming") behavior is even more appealing, since many services are provided for free (e.g., consumers frequently use several forms of social media or read many online newspapers).

23. We show that firms operating in media markets devote significant attention to the composition of their demand (i.e., the share of exclusive and multihoming consumers), while firms operating in more traditional markets essentially focus on total demand. In traditional markets, firms mostly derive revenues from consumers, who are all charged the same price, be they exclusive or multihoming consumers. Thus, firms mainly focus on total demand, and not the composition of the demand. Conversely, in two-sided media markets, firms mainly derive revenues from advertising. If advertisers are not willing to pay the same price for a first and a second impression, demand composition matters for firms' profits (i.e., multihoming consumers tend to be less valuable than exclusive ones). This can have important implications for firms' differentiation strategies. Indeed, the extent of product differentiation in a market is likely to affect consumers' incentives to purchase different products or services.

24. We show that if differentiation leads to an increase in the number of (less-valuable) multihoming consumers, firms operating in media markets will have limited incentives to differentiate. Conversely, since all consumers generate the same value in more traditional market, firms are mainly interested in the effect of differentiation on the total size of demand. In particular, if differentiation leads to market expansion, firms have incentives to differentiate. Importantly, we show that mergers can restore firms' incentives to differentiate in media markets, but that it comes at the cost of higher prices for advertisers.

25. In Chapter 2, we explore the merit of stricter disclosure rules, or minimum message length policy, in environments that involve an informed adviser and an uninformed decision maker. In many instances, the economic implications of our choices are surrounded by uncertainty. Consequently, we often rely on the advice of more informed parties to guide our choices. However, such parties may be biased toward one particular outcome, and decide to reveal only information favorable to their cause. This can raise suspicion as to the reliability of the information provided. Review platforms provide a nice example of such issues.

26. We consider a setting in which information is costly to disclose for the adviser, and this cost is private information. We show that the benefit of a stricter disclosure rule hinges on the (ex-ante) alignment of the parties' interests and the quality of the adviser's information. We notably show that the effect of the policy is less likely to be positive when the expertise of the adviser is high. We also explore the adviser's incentives to acquire more precise information and show how a more demanding disclosure policy affects those incentives.

27. In Chapter 3, we explore the strategic relations between integrated incumbents and a new entrant in the Chilean mobile telecommunications market. Before entry, three mobile network operators used to supply the market. The entry of a fourth operator had a huge impact on the market: prices fell and incumbents' market shares were dramatically affected. However, incumbents were asymmetrically affected by entry. Upon entry, the new operator had to rely on a network access contract to provide sufficient coverage to consumers.

28. We discuss how asymmetric cannibalization affects incentives to provide access. Intuitively, an incumbent that expects disproportionate cannibalization of its market share may have more incentives to provide access, since access revenues allows to partially recoup retail losses. However, we find evidence that retail losses are endogeneous to access provision. Indeed, we show that the access provider had less incentives to decrease its retail prices following entry. We use an empirical oligopoly model to rationalize a sudden decrease in retail prices that resulted from a change in access supplier.

References

Acquisti, A., Taylor, C., & Wagman, L. (2016). The economics of privacy. *Journal of economic Literature*, 54(2), 442-92.

Affeldt, P., Filistrucchi, L., & Klein, T. J. (2013). Upward pricing pressure in two-sided markets. *The Economic Journal*, 123(572), F505-F523.

Allcott, H., Braghieri, L., Eichmeyer, S., & Gentzkow, M. (2020). The welfare effects of social media. *American Economic Review*, 110(3), 629-76.

Anderson, S. P., & Coate, S. (2005). Market provision of broadcasting: A welfare analysis. *The review of Economic studies*, 72(4), 947-972.

Armstrong, M. (2006). Competition in two-sided markets. *The RAND journal of economics*, 37(3), 668-691.

Bacache, M., Bourreau, M., & Gaudin, G. (2014). Dynamic entry and investment in new infrastructures: Empirical evidence from the fixed broadband industry. *Review of Industrial Organization*, 44(2), 179-209.

Bail, C. A., Argyle, L. P., Brown, T. W., Bumpus, J. P., Chen, H., Hunzaker, M. F., Volfovsky, A. (2018). Exposure to opposing views on social media can increase political polarization. *Proceedings of the National Academy of Sciences*, 115(37), 9216-9221.

Barrett, Hendrix and Sims (2021), "Fueling the Fire: How Social Media Intensifies U.S. Political Polarization — And What Can Be Done About It."

Belleflamme, P., & Vergote, W. (2016). Monopoly price discrimination and privacy: The hidden cost of hiding. *Economics Letters*, 149, 141-144.

Belleflamme, P., & Peitz, M. (2015). Industrial organization: markets and strategies. Cambridge University Press.

Belleflamme, P., & Peitz, M. (2021). The Economics of Platforms. Cambridge University Press.

Biglaiser, G., Crémer, J., & Veiga, A. (2022). Should I stay or should I go? Migrating away from an incumbent platform. *The RAND Journal of Economics*, 53(3), 453-483.

Bourreau, M., (2016). Régulation des communications électroniques. Hermès Science publications.

Bourreau, M., Caillaud, B., & De Nijs, R. (2018). Taxation of a digital monopoly platform. *Journal of Public Economic Theory*, 20(1), 40-51.

Bourreau, M., Sun, Y., & Verboven, F. (2021). Market entry, fighting brands, and tacit collusion: Evidence from the French mobile telecommunications market. *American Economic Review*, 111(11), 3459-99.

Caillaud, B., & Jullien, B. (2003). Chicken & egg: Competition among intermediation service providers. *RAND journal of Economics*, 309-328.

Calvano, E., & Polo, M. (2020). Strategic differentiation by business models: Free-to-air and pay-tv. *The Economic Journal*, 130(625), 50-64.

Cave, M. (2006). Encouraging infrastructure competition via the ladder of investment. *Telecommunications Policy*, 30(3-4), 223-237.

Che, Y. K., & Hörner, J. (2018). Recommender systems as mechanisms for social learning. *The Quarterly Journal of Economics*, 133(2), 871-925.

Crémer, J., de Montjoye, Y.A., Schweitzer, H. (2019), Competition policy for the digital era.

Czernich, N., Falck, O., Kretschmer, T., & Woessmann, L. (2011). Broadband infrastructure and economic growth. *The Economic Journal*, 121(552), 505-532.

Evans, D. S., & Schmalensee, R. (2016). Matchmakers: The new economics of multisided platforms. *Harvard Business Review Press.*

Evans, D. S. (2003). The antitrust economics of multi-sided platform markets. *Yale J. on Reg.*, 20, 325.

Filistrucchi, L. (2008). A SSNIP test for two-sided markets: the case of media. Available at SSRN 1287442.

Furman, J. (2019), Unlocking digital competition, Report of the Digital Competition Expert Panel.

Featuring Online Customer Reviews: A Guide for Platforms (2022). Available at https://www.ftc.gov/busines guidance/advertising-marketing/endorsements-influencers-reviews.

Galeotti, A., & Moraga-González, J. L. (2009). Platform intermediation in a market for differentiated products. *European Economic Review*, 53(4), 417-428.

Gugler, K., Mueller, D. C., Yurtoglu, B. B., & Zulehner, C. (2003). The effects of mergers: an international comparison. *International journal of industrial organization*, 21(5), 625-653.

Halaburda, H., Jullien, B., & Yehezkel, Y. (2020). Dynamic competition with network externalities: how history matters. *The RAND Journal of Economics*, 51(1), 3-31.

Jeanjean, F., & Houngbonon, G. V. (2017). Market structure and investment in the mobile industry. *Information Economics and Policy*, 38, 12-22.

Jeon, D. S., & Choi, J. P. (2020). A leverage theory of tying in two-sided markets with non-negative price constraints. *American Economic Journal: Microeconomics.*

Jullien, B. (2011). Competition in multi-sided markets: Divide and conquer.*American Economic Journal: Microeconomics*, 3(4), 186-220.

Jullien, B., Lefouili, Y., & Riordan, M. H. (2020). Privacy Protection, Security, and Consumer Retention.

Jullien, B., & Sand-Zantman, W. (2021). The economics of platforms: A theory guide for competition policy.*Information Economics and Policy*, 54, 100880.

Laffont, J. J., & Tirole, J. (2001). Competition in telecommunications. MIT press.

Lazer, D. M., Baum, M. A., Benkler, Y., Berinsky, A. J., Greenhill, K. M., Menczer, F.,... & Zittrain, J. L. (2018). The science of fake news. *Science*, 359(6380), 1094-1096.

Lefouili, Y., & Toh, Y. L. (2022). Privacy and quality. TSE Working Paper 17 (795).

Montes, R., Sand-Zantman, W., Valletti, T. (2019). The value of personal information in online markets with endogenous privacy. *Management Science*, 65(3), 1342-1362.

Moraga-González, J. L., & Petrikaite˙, V. (2013). Search costs, demand-side economies, and the incentives to merge under Bertrand competition. *The RAND Journal of Economics*, 44(3), 391-424.

National roaming for resilience report, ENISA. Available at https://www.enisa.europa.eu/publications/nation roaming-for-resilience

Nicolle, A., Grzybowski, L., & Zulehner, C. (2018). Impact Of Competition, Investment, And Regulation On Prices Of Mobile Services: Evidence From France. *Economic Inquiry*, 56(2), 1322-1345.

OECD, *Keeping the Internet Up and Running in Times of Crisis*, 2020.

OECD, Digital Economy Outlook Supplement, *Digital Transformation in the Age of Covid-19*, 2020.

Rochet, J. C., & Tirole, J. (2003). Platform competition in two-sided markets. *Journal of the European Economic Association*, 1(4), 990-1029.

Rochet, J. C., & Tirole, J. (2006). Two-sided markets: a progress report. *The RAND journal of economics*, 37(3), 645-667. ISO 690

Seim, K., & Viard, V. B. (2011). The effect of market structure on cellular technology adoption and pricing. *American economic journal: Microeconomics*, 3(2), 221-51.

Stigler Committee on Digital Platforms (2019). Available at https://www.chicagobooth.edu/research/stigler/ and-media/committee-on-digital-platforms-final-report.

CHAPTER 1

PRODUCT DIFFERENTIATION WITH BUNDLES OF CHARACTERISTICS AND MULTIPURCHASING[1]

1.1 Introduction

29. **Motivation.** In many product markets, some consumers frequently purchase several competing products (multipurchasing) such as cars, magazines, or various electronic devices while others stick to one product (single-purchasing). For instance, some consumers decide to purchase both a laptop and a tablet, although the two products offer many similar characteristics. With the advent of the digital economy and the emergence of platforms, multipurchasing (or "multihoming") has become a widespread phenomenon (e.g., consumers frequently use several forms of social media or read many online newspapers), and it plays a key role in firms' profitability and strategies.[2]

30. Platforms are firms that operate in multisided markets, in which consumers' prices are often very low or even zero. This scenario makes purchasing several competing products or services even more attractive for consumers. Indeed, whereas video streaming services and car and electronic devices manufacturers essentially rely on consumers to derive revenues, online newspapers or social media often offer free services to consumers and charge advertisers to generate profits. However, the way multipurchasing affects firms that operate in one-sided markets (i.e., where firms mainly derive revenues from consumers) and

1 I am particularly indebted to Marc Bourreau for many discussions and thoughtful guidance throughout the writing of this paper. I am also grateful to Simon Anderson, Yann Balgobin, Alexandre de Cornière, François Jeanjean, Armando José Garcia Pires, Bruno Jullien, Yassine Lefouili, Nicolas Pasquier, Adrien Raizonville, Wilfried Sand-Zantman, and various participants at the Telecom Paris seminar on the Economics of Digitization, Jornadas de Economia Industrial (Madrid), Media Economics Workshop (Braga), AFREN 3EN (La Rochelle) and the 4th doctoral workshop on the Economics of Digitization (Toulouse) for many useful comments and suggestions.

2 In multisided (or two-sided) markets, consumers who use multiple horizontally differentiated services are usually called multihomers. We refer to this term when analyzing two-sided environments but use the term multipurchasing in one-sided settings.

two-sided markets (i.e., where firms may derive revenues from channels other than consumers) may differ.

31. In one-sided markets, firms may not care much about the composition of demand, whereas in two-sided environments, the composition of demand plays a key role. For instance, when considering advertising, exclusive eyeballs do not generate the same value as consumers who are active on multiple platforms. The bargaining power of platforms vis-a-vis advertisers is indeed affected by the extent of multipurchasing in the market.

32. One potential consequence may be an effect on the incentives for firms to differentiate from each other. Intuitively, a consumer's decision to purchase two horizontally differentiated products instead of one is related to the level of differentiation between those products. If differentiation leads to an increase in the number of (less-valuable) multihoming consumers, platforms may lack incentives to differentiate. Conversely, firms operating in one-sided markets may not care about multipurchasing since all types of consumers are typically charged the same price. This rationale may explain why video streaming services such as Netflix, which derive revenue mainly from consumers, choose to offer exclusive content (i.e., a high level of differentiation), while free online newspapers usually produce similar articles on their websites (i.e., a low level of differentiation).

33. **Model and results.** We build a model that highlights the main trade-offs discussed above. Specifically, we are interested in how the level of differentiation chosen by firms is affected by multipurchasing and the type of market considered, namely, one-sided or two-sided markets. Hotelling's model is the typical framework used to study competition between (two) horizontally differentiated firms.[3] Our framework relies on three important additional features.

34. First, we introduce the possibility for consumers to purchase either one product or service offered by one of the two firms or both firms' products or services. Multipurchasing arises endogenously in the model as a result of consumers' arbitrage between the benefit of purchasing a second product in addition to the first one and the costs to do so. The composition of each firm's demand is affected by the level of differentiation in the market and firms' prices.

35. Second, we develop a new way to model product differentiation, considering that firms can offer bundles of characteristics, represented by segments on the characteristic line. We consider that some characteristics are present in both

---

3 Salop (1979) and Chen and Riordan (2007) develop models of spatial differentiation with $n \geq 2$ firms.

firms' bundles, and firms can reduce the overlap in characteristics by offering more differentiated bundles. This in turn affects the incentives for consumers to purchase both products instead of one.

36. Last, we complement our analysis by considering a two-sided framework, where firms can also derive revenue from another source (e.g., advertising), and compare equilibrium outcomes with the standard one-sided setting. We also analyze how mergers affect firms incentives to differentiate in both settings.

37. Our results shed light on the influence of multipurchasing on firms' incentives to differentiate from each other. While the "principle of differentiation" (Tirole, 1988) relies on strategic interactions between firms' prices, we show that this result still holds in the absence of such interactions. In our setting, an increase in differentiation leads to a decrease in the overlap between firms' bundles of characteristics, which increases each firm's total demand.

38. More importantly, the impact of differentiation on demand composition is more ambiguous: we identify two countervailing effects of differentiation on demand composition. The *overlap-reducing* effect makes multipurchasing more attractive through an increase in the gross utility from consuming the two products, whereas the *segmentation effect* tends to segment the market through an increase in transportation costs. If consumers' heterogeneity is weak (i.e., transportation costs are relatively low), the former effect dominates the latter, and differentiation tends to stimulate multipurchasing behavior. However, in multisided markets, the value attributed to single-homers is typically larger than that attributed to multihomers. A direct consequence is that firms' incentives to differentiate may be dampened.

39. The analysis of mergers provides insightful results. While the result of maximum differentiation subsists in the one-sided environment, we show that a merger can overturn the result of minimum differentiation in the two-sided setting. This comes at the cost of higher prices for advertisers. Intuitively, a merger restores firms' bargaining power vis-à-vis advertisers since the merged entity becomes the unique gateway to multihoming consumers. As these consumers become more valuable, firms care less about demand composition and more about total demand, which increases in differentiation. Overall, mergers increase welfare, although advertisers' surplus is fully extracted.

40. **Related literature.** Our work contributes to several strands of the literature. The first strand is related to product differentiation. In Hotelling's seminal paper (1929), products are considered as single points in a characteristic space. Since then, most of the economic literature addressing horizontal product differentiation has considered products in this way. An important exception is Lancaster (1975), who uses a two-dimensional framework to define products. Closer to

our framework is that of Alexandrov (2008), who develops a model in which firms offer interval-long "fat" products on the Hotelling line. We also model products as intervals on the Hotelling line but allow consumers to purchase multiple products and introduce the idea that consumers may suffer from overlapping characteristics. This provides a new motivation for differentiation.

41. Another central element in models of spatial product differentiation is the assumption that consumers buy at most one product. Kim and Serfes (2006) allow consumers to buy one unit of each product and show that the usual result of maximum product differentiation (d'Aspremont et al., 1979) may no longer hold under multipurchasing. In our model, allowing for multipurchasing also entails strategic independence between firms' prices, which may dampen incentives to differentiate. However, when consumers suffer from overlapping characteristics, we show that firms can still have incentives to differentiate to enhance demand.

42. Our work is also related to the literature on two-sided markets and media markets in particular. Gabszewicz et al. (2001) and Anderson et al. (2018) both study how advertising affects firms' incentives to differentiate in a Hotelling setting. Gabszewicz et al. (2001) introduce advertising revenues in addition to revenues from consumers and find that the *demand effect* (i.e., firms' incentives to move toward the middle of the market to gain more captive consumers) can dominate the *strategic effect* (i.e., firms' incentives to move away from each other to escape price competition), leading to minimum differentiation at equilibrium. Their model maintains the assumption of single-homing consumers. Anderson et al. (2018) develop the incremental pricing principle, according to which multihoming consumers are less valuable than single-homing consumers due to decreasing returns to advertising. They find that firms are incentivized to move away from each other to increase the number of exclusive consumers and to prevent multihoming behavior. This effect is also at play in our model. However, we identify a countervailing force according to which differentiation can also increase the attractiveness of multihoming, leading to different implications. Our analysis suggests that the impact of differentiation on demand composition is more ambiguous than the standard Hotelling logic would indicate. We also emphasize how the importance of demand composition varies in one-sided and two-sided markets.

43. Finally, our work contributes to the literature studying the relation between market structure and diversity. Steiner (1952) predicts that competition leads to duplication of popular formats and that market concentration can solve this issue. Conversely, Spence and Owen (1977) find that monopoly may perform worse than competition in terms of variety provision. Johnson and Rhodes (2021) study quality competition between multiproduct firms and find that mergers induce a change in the mix of different qualities offered

by firms, which can benefit consumers. On the empirical side, several contributions have shown that ownership concentration can lead to increased diversity in media markets (Berry and Waldfogel, 2001; George, 2007; Sweeting, 2010). Fan (2013) insists on the importance of accounting for product characteristics choices to assess the welfare impact of a merger. She finds that mergers lead to less variety. Gentzkow et al. (2014) highlight the importance of markets' two-sidedness in evaluating competition policy. They argue that advertising collusion increases both welfare and diversity. Finally, Jeziorski (2014) finds that advertisers are negatively affected by mergers, while consumers are positively affected and benefit from greater diversity. Our results are consistent with the latter findings: we show that mergers hurt advertisers but are likely to foster firms' incentives to differentiate. We unveil a new mechanism as to why mergers may increase diversity.

44. **Organization of the paper.** In the following section, we develop a model of horizontal differentiation with bundles of characteristics, which allows us to introduce our main novel effect, i.e., that differentiation may encourage multipurchasing. Section 3.1 is devoted to the analysis in a one-sided environment, while Section 3.2 addresses the two-sided scenario. We conduct welfare analysis in Section 4. In Section 5, we analyze the impact of mergers in both types of environments. Finally, Section 6 concludes.

1.2 A model of horizontal differentiation with bundles of characteristics

45. **Firms.** Consider two firms that each produce one good. Each good is composed of different characteristics. The set of characteristics that can be incorporated into the goods is represented by a line with unit length, where each point of the line represents one characteristic.

46. When designing their good, firms choose a bundle of characteristics to incorporate, which corresponds to a segment of fixed size q on the characteristic line.[4] We define the location of each firm's good, a and b, as the middle point of the segment chosen on the characteristic line. We let $a \leq \frac{1}{2}$ and $b \geq \frac{1}{2}$. For ease of exposition, we assume that firms choose their locations; therefore,

4 This modeling approach is consistent with the description provided by Spence (1976): "One can think of products being points in a continuous spectrum of attributes. The market selects a finite subset of points in the continuum, these being the products actually produced". Note also that Lancaster (1975) describes products as "bundles of characteristics".

the bounds of the characteristics' segments are defined as $\left[a-\frac{q}{2}, a+\frac{q}{2}\right]$ for firm 1's good and $\left[b-\frac{q}{2}, b+\frac{q}{2}\right]$ for firm 2's good. The overlap in product characteristics is given by the intersection between the two characteristic segments: $O = max(q - (b - a), 0)$. The overlap O is weakly decreasing in product differentiation (i.e., $b - a$).

47. To keep the analysis simple, we assume that firm 1 and firm 2's location choices are restricted to the intervals $\left[\frac{1-q}{2}, \frac{1}{2}\right]$ and $\left[\frac{1}{2}, \frac{1+q}{2}\right]$, respectively. This simply implies that firms choose the overlap between their products, which ranges between full overlap $\left(a=b=\frac{1}{2}, O=q\right)$ to zero overlap $\left(a=\frac{1-q}{2}, b=\frac{1+q}{2}, O=0\right)$. This assumption ensures strategic interactions between the two firms.[5]

48. **Consumers.** Consumers are uniformly distributed over the line. A consumer's preferred bundle is defined by the following segment on the characteristic line, $\left[x-\frac{q}{2}, x+\frac{q}{2}\right]$, where x denotes a consumer's type.[6] Consumers therefore exhibit some heterogeneity in the correspondence between their preferences and firms' products offerings, in the Hotelling spirit. To allow for demand expansion, we assume that the market is not fully covered ($q < \frac{t}{4}$ is a sufficient condition).

49. Purchasing a given product i provides two types of characteristics to the consumer: characteristics that exactly correspond to what she expects to find in her optimal good and other characteristics that do not correspond to her preferences. Denoting as δ the set of characteristics that meet the consumer's preferences and μ as the set of other characteristics, we let the (gross) utility a consumer x derives from purchasing product i be:

$$U_i^x = \delta_i^x + k\mu_i^x,$$

5 Absent this assumption, firms could consider locating so far away from each other that they would potentially behave as local monopolies. Relaxing this assumption would not affect our results in the one-sided analysis but would make the two-sided analysis less clear-cut. Note that this restriction arises due to our assumption of uniform consumer distribution and would be less likely to be necessary with a unimodal consumer density, centered about $\frac{1}{2}$. Another way to consider this restriction on feasible locations would be to assume an increasing, convex, and sufficiently high cost to differentiate.

6 This specification implies that consumers perfectly know the quality standards in the market (i.e., q is common knowledge) and derive their optimal bundle accordingly.

where $k \in [0, 1]$ represents the relative preference for preferred characteristics. If consumer x decides to purchase product j in addition to product i, we define her utility as:

$$U_{ij}^{x} = \delta_i^x + \delta_j^x + k(\mu_i^x + \mu_j^x) - \alpha O,$$

where α represents the extent to which consumers dislike overlapping characteristics.[7] Figure 1 illustrates the single-purchasing and multipurchasing cases.

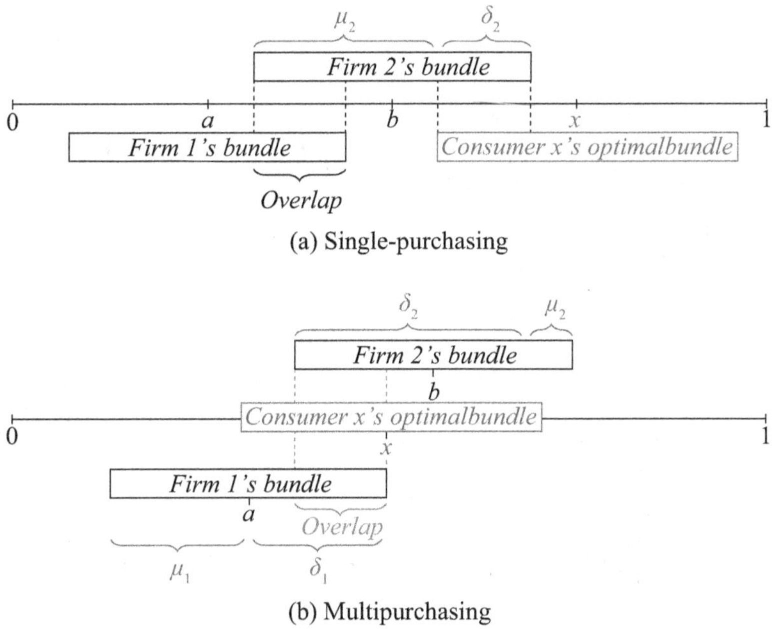

Figure 1.1: Consumer's utility with bundles of characteristics.

50. The timing that we consider throughout the paper is as follows. In the first period, firms choose their locations and therefore the bundle of characteristics they offer. In the second period, firms choose prices; then, demand is realized. We use subgame perfection as a solution concept.

7 This modeling approach is reminiscent of Anderson et al. (2017), who consider a Hotelling setting where firms can invest in some vertical quality dimension and some characteristics may end-up being present in both products. However, in their model, the overlap in product characteristics is independent of the locations (which are fixed). This scenario implies that two differentiated goods can incur each characteristic of the universe with the same probability. By contrast, we assume that characteristics are the element that defines the level of differentiation of firms. As a consequence, the overlap in product characteristics is decreasing in product differentiation and can therefore be controlled by firms.

51. Before turning to the analysis of the model, we show that our utility functions are similar to the standard Hotelling framework. To see this, first note that μ_i^x is proportional to the distance (d_i) between the consumer's and the firm's locations. Additionally, keeping in mind that the size of the bundle is equal to q, we can rewrite $\delta_i^x = q - d_i$. Substituting for these values in U_i^x yields $U_i = q - d_i + kd_i$. Finally, define $t = 1 - k$, with $t \in [0, 1]$, which gives us the consumer utility function (net of price):

$$U_i = q - td_i - p_i. \tag{1.1}$$

52. With our simple framework, we are therefore able to derive the standard Hotelling utility function, where q can be viewed as the standard stand-alone benefit and t can be interpreted as the extent to which consumers dislike unexpected characteristics. Note that this transformation assumes that consumers who cannot obtain any of their desired characteristics (i.e., are located too far from the firms) do not consider buying the good.[8]

53. The interest of our framework arises in the multipurchasing case. Applying the above reasoning to the multipurchasing case, we obtain:

$$U_{ij} = q_i + q_j - t(d_i + d_j) - (p_i + p_j) - \alpha O. \tag{1.2}$$

54. The main objective of the framework developed above is to demonstrate why the incremental utility may be closely related to the level of differentiation in the market.[9] As we shall see below, this finding implies that multipurchasing can become more attractive for consumers when firms are located further apart, an effect that has not been raised in the literature thus far and has important implications for firms' differentiation strategies. In what follows, we use equations (1) and (2) to derive consumers' demand functions and firms' optimal strategies in one-sided and two-sided settings.

1.3 Analysis

1.3.1 One-sided environment

55. In this subsection, we analyze firms' price and differentiation decisions when they derive revenues exclusively from the price they charge to consumers. In Subsection 3.2, we show how equilibrium outcomes are affected when firms also derive revenues from another source (e.g., advertising).

8 Our results would be qualitatively similar in a more standard Hotelling setting, assuming that the incremental utility is simply an increasing function of the level of differentiation in the market. The characteristics approach provides an innovative rationale as to why this might be the case.

9 Our model's philosophy is remarkably close to the description provided by Lancaster (1975): "The consumer obtains his optimal bundle of characteristics by purchasing a collection of goods so chosen as to possess *in toto* the desired characteristics".

56. ***Demand.*** As discussed above, each firm's demand can be composed of single-purchasers and multipurchasers. The more preferred product for a consumer is the closer one. The extreme part of firms' demands is determined by the consumer who is indifferent between purchasing good i or not purchasing anything ($u_{i0} = 0$):

$$x_{10} = a - \frac{1}{t}(q - p_1), \tag{1.3}$$

$$x_{20} = b + \frac{1}{t}(q - p_2). \tag{1.4}$$

57. The interior part of each firm i's demand is determined by the consumer who is indifferent between purchasing only product j ($j \neq i$) and purchasing both products i and j: $u_j = u_{jM}$, which yields:

$$x_{1M} = b - \frac{1}{t}[q - \alpha O - p_2]. \tag{1.5}$$

$$x_{2M} = a + \frac{1}{t}[q - \alpha O - p_1].^{10} \tag{1.6}$$

58. Figure 2 shows the demand configuration and consumers' indirect utilities.[11]

59. Total demands D_1 and D_2 are obtained by combining (3)-(6) for firm 1 (i.e., $x_{2M} - x_{10}$) and (4)-(5) for firm 2 (i.e., $x_{20} - x_{1M}$):

$$D_1 = \frac{1}{t}[2q - \alpha O - 2p_1], \tag{1.7}$$

$$D_2 = \frac{1}{t}[2q - \alpha O - 2p_2]. \tag{1.8}$$

60. Note that firms' total demands depend only on their own prices. This is a standard property of horizontal differentiation models with multipurchasing.[12] More importantly, each firm's demand is increasing in differentiation for $(b - a) \in [0, q]$. An increase in differentiation reduces the overlap between firms' characteristics, which makes purchasing the two goods instead of only one more attractive for consumers located in the middle of the market.[13] In one-sided settings, all consumers generate the same value. Thus, only the

10 For $b - a = q$ or $\alpha = 0$, each firm's left and right wings are thus determined in the same way.

11 Multipurchasers all obtain the same utility from purchasing the two products. Note that they all face the same transportation costs to buy from both firms due to our linear specification of transportation costs. If we assumed quadratic costs instead, utilities would be higher for multipurchasers located closer to 0.

12 See Kim and Serfes (2006) or Anderson et al. (2017, 2019). Similarly, in Ambrus et al. (2016), firms' total demands depend only on their own advertising level (consumers are not charged anything but are subject to advertising).

13 That differentiation can lead to market expansion is supported by both early theoretical predictions (Steiner, 1952) and empirical findings (Berry and Waldfogel, 1999). Nonetheless, this effect is usually absent in models of horizontal differentiation.

total demand matters for profit maximization. We defer the analysis of demand composition to Section 3.2.

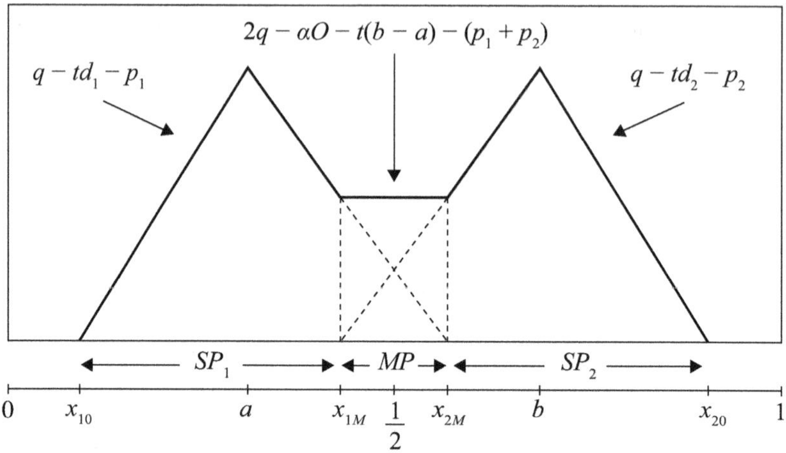

Figure 1.2: Demand structure and indirect utilities.

61. ***Prices.*** In a one-sided environment, each firm $i = 1, 2$ maximizes its profit:

$$\pi_i = p_i D_i = \frac{p_i}{t}[2q - \alpha O - 2p_i]. \tag{1.9}$$

62. Indeed, consumers are all charged the same price, be they single-purchasers or multipurchasers. Taking the first-order condition with respect to p_i leads to:

$$p_i^* = \frac{1}{4}[2q - \alpha O]. \tag{1.10}$$

63. Note that as firms' demand (and therefore profits) depend only on their own prices, the best response functions and equilibrium prices (for given location choices) coincide. Furthermore, optimal prices are increasing in differentiation.

64. ***Location choice.*** In the first stage of the game, each firm $i = 1, 2$ maximizes the profit function $\pi_i(p_i^*)$, where is given in (10). Taking the derivative with respect to location yields:

$$\frac{\partial \pi_i}{\partial d} = \frac{\alpha}{4t}[2q - \alpha O] > 0,$$

where $d = -a, b$. Since $\frac{\partial \pi_i}{\partial d} > 0$, firms have incentive to differentiate as much as possible, leading to maximum differentiation in equilibrium.

65. **Proposition 1:** *In the one-sided setting where firms derive revenue only from consumers and consumers suffer from overlapping characteristics (i.e., $\alpha > 0$), maximum differentiation arises in equilibrium. Equilibrium prices and demands are, respectively, given by* $p_1^* = p_2^* = \frac{q}{2}$ *and* $D_1^* = D_2^* = \frac{q}{t}$.[14]

66. This result is in line with the "principle of differentiation" (Tirole, 1988); however, the reasons this result emerges in the present context are different. In standard models of horizontal differentiation, the strategic effect of differentiation on firms' prices is so strong that firms decide to locate as far as possible from each other. In our model, there is no strategic interaction between firms' prices, as already noted. The result arises because each firm's total demand is strictly increasing in differentiation, provided that $\alpha > 0$.

67. The absence of strategic interaction between firms' prices allows us to focus on demand-related incentives to engage in differentiation. Surprisingly, our results sharply contrast with the existing literature (Kim and Serfes, 2006; Anderson et al., 2018), which suggests that minimum differentiation arises when prices are strategically independent and all types of consumers generate the same value to the firms. Our analysis emphasizes the role of demand expansion in predicting market outcomes.

68. ***Special case with*** $\alpha = 0$**.** When $\alpha = 0$, consumers do not suffer from overlapping characteristics and therefore fully enjoy each firm's bundle. Intuitively, this may disincentivize firms from locating far from each other. Indeed, when $\alpha = 0$, firm *i*'s demand simply becomes:

$$D_i = \frac{2}{t}(q - p_i). \tag{1.11}$$

69. A firm's total demand is therefore independent of its location. Taking the first-order condition with respect to price, we obtain: $p_i^* = \frac{q}{2}$. As mentioned above, demand is independent of location, as are prices. Firms are therefore indifferent in regards to where to locate; however, one could assume that firms have to incur a small nonzero cost to engage in differentiation. If so, we obtain the following result.

70. **Proposition 2:** *When* $\alpha = 0$*, consumers do not suffer from overlapping characteristics and firms' demands are independent of their location. In the one-sided setting where firms derive all revenue from consumers, minimum differentiation arises when there is a small nonzero cost to engage in differentiation.*

---

14 Any pair of locations that satisfy $(b - a) = q$ forms an equilibrium. Thus, there exist a symmetric equilibrium and a continuum of asymmetric equilibria that satisfy this requirement and lead to the same equilibrium prices and demands.

71. Note that we could also assume away any cost of differentiation and stick to the result of indifferent location. Notably, this special case highlights that the only incentive for firms to move away from their competitor is to reduce the overlap between the characteristics they offer, which increases total demand.

1.3.2 Multisided environment

72. We analyze a situation in which consumers are not charged anything by firms. This situation is consistent with platforms' strategies often observed in digital or media markets.[15] There is a unit mass of advertisers who are willing to place ads on the platform. Similar to Anderson et al. (2018, 2019) and Ambrus et al. (2016), we assume that advertisers are willing to pay r per ad for a unique impression and σr for a second impression, where $\sigma \in [0, 1]$. Thus, reaching the same consumer a second time is worth (weakly) less than reaching them for the first time. The extent of multihoming constitutes a measure of competition intensity in the market: a multihoming consumer can be reached by advertisers through both platforms. Under competition, each platform can charge σr for each multihoming consumer.[16] In line with the literature, we further assume that advertisers place only one ad per platform. Since multihoming consumers tend to generate less revenue than single-homing consumers, we start by analyzing how differentiation affects demand composition.

73. ***Demand composition.*** To obtain the single-homers part (SP_i) of firms' demands, we combine equations (3)-(5) for firm 1 (i.e., $x_{1M} - x_{10}$) and equations (4)-(6) for firm 2 (i.e., $x_{20} - x_{2M}$):

$$SP_1 = [b - a]\left(1 - \frac{\alpha}{t}\right) - \frac{1}{t}[p_1 - p_2] + \frac{\alpha}{t}q, \tag{1.12}$$

$$SP_2 = [b - a]\left(1 - \frac{\alpha}{t}\right) - \frac{1}{t}[p_2 - p_1] + \frac{\alpha}{t}q. \tag{1.13}$$

74. The number of consumers who multihome ($MP = x_{2M} - x_{1M}$) is given by:

$$MP = [b - a]\left(\frac{2\alpha}{t} - 1\right) - \frac{(p_1 + p_2)}{t} + \frac{2q}{t}(1 - \alpha). \tag{1.14}$$

75. Interestingly, differentiation has an ambiguous effect on the composition of demand. An increase in differentiation entails two opposite effects: a *segmentation* effect and an *overlap-reducing* effect. To see how these effects operate, assume first that $\alpha = 0$, such that the *overlap-reducing* effect is not at play.

15 In the main text, we focus on polar cases where firms derive revenues from consumers or from advertising. This scenario makes the exposition clearer. In the Appendix, we develop the case in which firms obtain revenue from both consumers and firms. This situation can be seen as an intermediate case. The main driving forces we identify in Subsections 3.1 and 3.2 still operate, but they are weighted against one another. Note that we provide the general formulas (12)-(14) with prices when we describe demand composition below but then conduct the analysis assuming away any price.

16 In Section 5, we discuss how this finding is affected if platforms merge.

In this case, an increase in differentiation implies a proportional shift in demand. For instance, if firm 2 moves away from its competitor, x_{1M} and x_{20} shift to the right. This mechanically implies a decrease in the number of multihoming consumers and an increase in the number of exclusive consumers; in other words, the market becomes more segmented. This is essentially what occurs in Anderson et al. (2018).

76. Consider now $\alpha > 0$. An increase in differentiation implies a proportional shift in x_{20} but a nonproportional change in x_{1M}. This difference is due to the *overlap-reducing* effect, which acts as a countervailing effect to the *segmentation* effect (hence, the increase in the firm's total demand). To see how the composition of firm *i*'s demand evolves with differentiation, one must consider x_{iM}. If firm 2 moves away from its competitor, it reduces the overlap between products' characteristics, which induces an increase in x_{2M}. In other words, firm 2 makes purchasing firm 1's product (on top of firm 2's product) more attractive. The extent of this effect is limited by the size of transportation costs (t) since multihoming also becomes more costly when firm 2 moves away from firm 1. Regardless, if the *overlap-reducing* effect is sufficiently large, the number of single-homing consumers decreases with differentiation while the number of multihoming consumers increases. Conversely, if transportation costs are large, the *segmentation* effect dominates the *overlap-reducing* effect, which implies that differentiation leads to more exclusive consumers and fewer multihoming consumers in the market.

77. Our analysis suggests that if consumer heterogeneity is strong, the market is more likely to be segmented. To illustrate the main forces at play, consider the media industry. One instance in which the *segmentation* effect presumably outweighs the *overlap-reducing* effect is when consumers have strong political views/bias. In such a case, differentiation between content (or media slanting) is likely to segment the market. It is rather infrequent for a consumer who watches CNN to also spend time on Fox News, although the two channels arguably broadcast different types of programs. This phenomenon is frequently referred to as *affective polarization*. Conversely, in the market for popular sports, consumers are less likely to exhibit any particular bias (i.e., there is less strong heterogeneity between consumers[17]) and appear to mainly be interested in content proposed by channels. This scenario suggests that differentiation (e.g., in the form of exclusive broad-casting of a particular sport or competition) tends to induce an increase in multihoming behavior. This reasoning is consistent with the analysis of the newspaper market conducted by Mullainathan and Shleifer (2005), who suggest that a high level of consumer heterogeneity (bias) leads to substantial media slanting, which segments the market. Conversely, a conscientious reader

17 Naturally, some consumers may be more interested in basketball and others in football, but it is less likely that consumers who like basketball also hate football. The same argument applies for video streaming services, whereby exclusive content tends to induce multihoming behavior, although some consumers may prefer Netflix and others Amazon Prime Video.

(unbiased) will tend to read both newspapers when newspapers slant in opposite directions. In other words, differentiation makes multihoming attractive to an unbiased reader. The following lemma summarizes the above discussion.

78. **Lemma 1**: *Differentiation affects demand composition as follows:*

- *For $\alpha > t$: SP_1 and SP_2 are decreasing in differentiation and MP is increasing in differentiation.*
- *For $\frac{t}{2} < \alpha < t$: SP_1, SP_2 and MP are all increasing in differentiation.*
- *For $\alpha < \frac{t}{2}$: SP_1 and SP_2 are increasing in differentiation and MP is decreasing in differentiation.*

79. ***Location choice.*** The profit function of platform i is given by:

$$\pi_i = rSP_i + \sigma rMP, \tag{1.15}$$

where SP_i and MP are taken with $p_i = 0$. Since we assume a free service for consumers, each platform maximizes its profit function with respect to only location. The first-order condition is given by:

$$\frac{\partial \pi_i}{\partial d} = 0 \Leftrightarrow r\left(1 - \frac{\alpha}{t}\right) + \sigma r\left(\frac{2\alpha}{t} - 1\right) = 0 \tag{1.16}$$

80. From Lemma 1, it immediately follows that the derivative can be either positive or negative. For intermediate values of α (i.e., $\frac{t}{2} < \alpha < t$), both terms in (16) are positive, so maximum differentiation unambiguously arises. In the two other cases stated in Lemma 1, the analysis is more ambiguous. Indeed, when $\alpha > t$, the left term of equation (16) is negative, whereas the right term is positive (i.e., SP_i decreases and MP increases in differentiation). Conversely, when $\alpha < \frac{t}{2}$, the left term is positive, whereas the right term is negative (i.e., SP_i increases and MP decreases in differentiation). However, in the latter case, the first effect always dominates the second effect, for every value of σ. As for the former case, which effect dominates depends on the value of σ. Proposition 3 below states the main results.

81. **Proposition 3:** *In the two-sided setting, where firms derive revenue only from advertising and consumers suffer from overlapping characteristics (i.e., $\alpha > 0$), firms optimal differentiation strategies are defined as follows:*

- *If $\alpha < t$, maximum differentiation arises for every value of σ;*

– *If $\alpha > t$, minimum differentiation arises provided that* $\sigma < \tilde{\sigma} = \dfrac{\frac{\alpha}{t} - 1}{\frac{2\alpha}{t} - 1}$, *and maximum differentiation arises otherwise.*

82. When σ is relatively low ($\sigma < \tilde{\sigma}$), firms derive much greater profits from single-homers than multihomers and thus care about how product differentiation may affect the number of single-homers in the market. In this case, when the *overlap-reducing* effect is strong ($\alpha > t$), minimum differentiation arises. Conversely, when the *segmentation* effect dominates ($\alpha < t$), maximum differentiation always arises (for all σ).

83. As σ increases, platforms care more about total demand and less about the composition of demand. When $\sigma = 1$, we end up in a similar situation as that in the one-sided setting, where single-homers and multihomers generate the same value. In this case, as total demand is strictly increasing in product differentiation, it is always profitable for firms to differentiate (i.e., maximum differentiation ensues).

84. The idea that advertising-financed markets can result in insufficient differentiation has already been raised in the literature.[18] In our setting, minimum differentiation also occurs as a result of firms' objective to maximize advertising revenues. However, we unveil a new mechanism that dampens firms' incentives to differentiate, namely, the evolution of demand composition. When we consider multihoming contexts, and differentiation affects demand composition, firms may refrain from engaging in differentiation. The reason is that if differentiation makes multihoming more attractive, firms' bargaining power vis-à-vis advertisers does not improve.[19] This is a stark difference with Anderson et al. (2018), who find that firms maximally differentiate if multihomers generate much less revenue than exclusive consumers. In our setting, an increase in differentiation does not necessarily segment the market.

85. ***Special case with*** $\alpha = 0$. As underlined previously, when $\alpha = 0$, consumers do not suffer from overlapping characteristics and firms' total demands become independent of the overlap and location. However, the composition of demand is not independent of location. As observed directly from (16), an increase in

---

18 Gabszewicz et al. (2001) revisit the standard Hotelling framework by introducing advertising revenues and show that firms may prefer to locate in the center of the market to secure the highest possible demand (even if this leads to the standard Bertrand paradox on the consumer side). The authors worry that advertising-financed markets may lead to the ascent of the "Pensée Unique".

19 Mullainathan and Shleifer (2005) predict that "when potential audiences share similar beliefs, we do not expect to see diversity of media reports". This corresponds to our prediction that when consumer heterogeneity is relatively small (i.e., the *overlap-reducing* effect dominates the *segmentation* effect), firms have limited incentives to engage in differentiation since it would stimulate multihoming and deteriorate their bargaining power vis-à-vis advertisers.

differentiation implies an increase in the number of single-homers for each firm and a proportional decrease in the number of multihomers (leaving total demand unchanged). We can therefore state the following proposition.

86. **Proposition 4:** *When $\alpha = 0$, the composition of demand is affected by location choice: an increase in differentiation implies an increase in the number of single-homers and a proportional decrease in the number of multihomers. In the two-sided setting, where firms derive revenue only from advertising, maximum differentiation arises when $\sigma < 1$.*

87. When $\alpha = 0$, the total demand functions are fixed, but firms can perfectly control their demand composition through differentiation. Since exclusive consumers are more valuable than multihoming consumers, firms maximally differentiate to reduce the number of multihoming consumers.[20]

88. The results obtained in this section highlight the difference between one-sided and two-sided settings. In the one-sided setting, firms only care about the total demand, which implies that they do not have incentive to differentiate if $\alpha = 0$. When α increases, firms' incentives to differentiate also increase (since total demand increases in differentiation for $\alpha > 0$). In the two-sided setting, the reasoning is reversed: when α is very large ($\alpha > t$), firms do not have incentives to differentiate (provided that σ is not excessively large) since this would imply a decrease in the number of exclusive consumers. However, as α starts to decrease, and at the extreme when $\alpha = 0$, an increase in differentiation unambiguously leads to more exclusive consumers in the market, which benefits firms (as long as $\sigma < 1$). We conclude that the way consumer disutility from overlapping characteristics affects firms' incentives for differentiation greatly depends on the type of market considered.

1.4 Welfare analysis

89. Total welfare is defined as the sum of consumer surplus and firms' profits. We begin the analysis with the one-sided scenario. To find the socially optimal outcome, one can abstract from prices, which are simply transfers between firms and consumers. Hence, total welfare is given by:

$$W = \int_{x_{10}}^{x_{1m}} (q - t\,|\,x - a\,|)\,dx + \int_{x_{1m}}^{x_{2m}} (2q - \alpha O - t(b - a))dx + \int_{x_{2m}}^{x_{20}} (q - t\,|\,x - b\,|)\,dx.$$

20 Again, this situation is particularly similar to that of Anderson et al. (2018), in which firm also perfectly control their demand composition and maximum differentiation arises when second impressions are worthless (i.e., $\sigma = 0$). Our main contribution is to consider situations where $\alpha > 0$ (i.e., the *overlap-reducing* effect kicks in), which makes the impact of differentiation on demand composition more ambiguous.

90. The way differentiation affects welfare is driven by the value of α with respect to t (i.e., the *overlap-reducing* effect vs the *segmentation* effect). When $\alpha > t$, the surplus associated with single-purchasers is decreasing in differentiation: the number of single-purchasing consumers decreases. Conversely, the surplus associated to multipurchasers increases: the number of multipurchasers increases, as does the utility they derive. When $\alpha < t$, the surplus associated with single-purchasers increases, and the surplus associated to multipurchasers tends to be negatively affected by differentiation.[21]

91. Taking the derivative of (17) with respect to location yields:

$$\frac{\partial W}{\partial d} = \frac{\alpha[qt + 2q(1-\alpha) + 2(a-b)(t-\alpha)]}{t}.$$

92. If $\alpha > t$, all terms in the numerator are positive; if $\alpha < t$, the last term becomes negative. This result reflects the lower utility that multipurchasers obtain when differentiation increases. However, we find that overall, total welfare always increases in differentiation. This result is driven by the demand expansion induced by differentiation. The equilibrium outcome therefore corresponds to the socially optimal one. Moreover, for consumer surplus, we have:

$$CS = \int_{x_{10}}^{x_{1m}} (q - t\,|\,x-a\,| - p_1)dx + + \int_{x_{1m}}^{x_{2m}} (2q - \alpha O - t(b-a) - (p_1 + p_2))dx + \int_{x_{2m}}^{x_{20}} (q - t\,|\,x-b\,| - p_2)dx.$$

93. The analysis of consumer surplus is more ambiguous. Indeed, while differentiation leads to market expansion, it also implies an increase in equilibrium prices. Integrating and taking the derivative with respect to location yields:

$$\frac{\partial CS}{\partial d} = \frac{2q(2+4t-5\alpha)\alpha - 2(b-a)(8t-5\alpha)\alpha}{8t}.$$

94. This expression is positive and decreasing in differentiation, which suggests that consumer surplus is increasing in differentiation up to a certain point. When $b - a = q$, the expression equals 0 for $t = \frac{1}{2}$ and is negative for higher values of t. Thus, the equilibrium outcome yields excessive differentiation from the consumers' perspective when $t > \frac{1}{2}$.

21 Specifically, when $\frac{t}{2} < \alpha < t$, the number of multipurchasers increases, but the utility they derive decreases in differentiation. When $\alpha < \frac{t}{2}$, the number of multipurchasers and their utility both decrease in differentiation.

95. Turning to the multisided analysis, total welfare is given by:

$$\begin{aligned} W = r[SP_1 + SP_2 + MP] + \sigma rMP + \int_{x_{10}}^{x_{1m}} (q - t| x - a |)dx \\ + \int_{x_{1m}}^{x_{2m}} (2q - \alpha O - t(b - a))dx + \int_{x_{2m}}^{x_{20}} (q - t| x - b |)dx. \end{aligned} \tag{1.18}$$

96. The first two terms jointly represent platforms' profits and advertisers' surplus, while the subsequent terms represent consumer surplus.[22] Note that consumer surplus corresponds to the total welfare studied in the one-sided case above; therefore, consumer surplus is always increasing in differentiation. In terms of platforms' and advertisers' (joint) surplus, it is overall increasing in differentiation. Indeed, total market demand is increasing in differentiation, such that the first term is always positive. Even in cases where the number of multipurchasers is decreasing in differentiation, it cannot offset the demand expansion effect. We deduce that the equilibrium outcome is not always aligned with the social optimum: our main results are summarized in Proposition 5.

97. **Proposition 5:** *In the one-sided setting, the equilibrium outcome coincides with the social optimum; however, consumer surplus is nonmonotonic in differentiation. When* $t > \frac{1}{2}$*, the equilibrium outcome features excessive differentiation from a consumer surplus perspective. In the two-sided setting, maximum differentiation is also socially desirable, and consumer surplus strictly increases in differentiation. Thus, from a social perspective, there is insufficient differentiation when* $\alpha > t$ *and* $\sigma < \tilde{\sigma}$.

1.5 Mergers

98. In this section, we analyze how mergers affect firms' differentiation strategies in one-sided and two-sided environments. There is an ongoing debate in competition policy as to whether one should treat mergers involving multisided businesses in the same way as those involving standard one-sided businesses. Our analysis sheds light on the way firms' incentives to differentiate can be affected in multi-sided vs one-sided contexts.

99. **One-sided environment.** We start by analyzing how firms' incentives to differentiate are affected in one-sided settings. As shown in Section 3.1, each

22 Competition prevents platforms from extracting the full value generated by multihomers. Advertisers are willing to pay up to $(r + \sigma r)$ for each multihoming consumer but end up paying only $2\sigma r$; their net surplus is thus $(r - \sigma r)MP$. The sum of platforms' profits is $r(SP_1 + SP_2) + 2\sigma rMP$. As we illustrate in the next section, a merger between the two platforms restores their ability to fully extract surplus from advertisers.

firm's total demand is strictly increasing in differentiation over the relevant interval. Since single-purchasers and multipurchasers generate the same value, firms always choose to differentiate. In this context, we find that a merger (to create a multi-product monopoly) will also lead to maximum differentiation.

100. As discussed above, differentiation is not driven by strategic interactions between prices in our model. Prices are strategically independent, so equilibrium prices are the same in a multiproduct monopoly and under competition. However, even if the equilibrium differentiation level is the same as that under competition, incentives to differentiate are strengthened post-merger. The merged entity maximizes $\Pi_{1+2} = p_1D_1 + p_2D_2$. Plugging in the optimal prices computed in 3.1 and taking the first-order condition with respect to location yields $\frac{\partial \Pi_{1+2}}{\partial d} = \frac{\alpha}{2t}[2q - \alpha O] > 0$. This expression is twice as large as $\frac{\partial \Pi_i}{\partial d}$.

101. Indeed, while the rival's price does not affect a firm's demand, each firm exerts an externality on the other firm through its location choice. As highlighted earlier, by moving toward the extreme, a firm reduces the overlap in product characteristics and makes its rival's product more attractive. A merger allows firms to internalize this effect.

102. **Two-sided environment.** The most striking effect we find relates to multisided mergers. The profit function of the merged entity is defined as $\tilde{\Pi} = r(SP_1 + SP_2 + MP) + \sigma r(MP)$. The main difference with competition is that the merged entity is able to derive a revenue $r + \sigma r$ for each multihoming consumer, as opposed to $2\sigma r$ under competition. Taking the derivative with respect to location leads to:

$$\frac{\partial \tilde{\Pi}_{1+2}}{\partial d} = r + \sigma r\left(\frac{2\alpha}{t} - 1\right). \tag{1.19}$$

103. The merger induces each platform to internalize the effect of differentiation on the whole market size (SP_1, SP_2, $M\,P$). Total market size is increasing in differentiation as a result of the decrease in characteristics overlap. Beyond total demand, platforms also care particularly about multipurchasers since a second impression generates additional revenue σr for the merged entity. Overall, we find that differentiation always increases firms' joint profit.

104. **Proposition 6:** *In one-sided settings, firms maximally differentiate in equilibrium regardless of market structure. In two-sided settings, equilibrium location strategies are affected by a merger. A merger induces maximum differentiation regardless of the value of* σ *and enhances social welfare when* $\alpha > t$ *and* $\sigma < \tilde{\sigma}$.

105. Proposition 6 shows that the minimum differentiation outcome that arises under competition (Proposition 3) is overturned when a merger occurs. The merger induces platforms to care about total market demand. Differentiation always leads to an increase in total demand, which is associated with additional revenue r. If the number of multihoming consumers is increasing in differentiation, the effect of differentiation on profits is unambiguously positive. If the number of multihoming consumers is decreasing in differentiation, differentiation also has a negative effect. However, the latter effect does not offset the first since the value of a second impression is (by definition) lower than that of the first impression (i.e., $\sigma \in [0, 1]$).

106. Our results suggest that mergers in two-sided environments are likely to be more beneficial from a welfare standpoint than mergers in one-sided environments. Indeed, in one-sided settings, firms always have an incentive to differentiate to expand market size, whereas in two-sided settings, firms care about demand composition and lack incentives to differentiate when they expect that differentiation is unlikely to lead to an increase in exclusive consumers. In this context, a merger can restore a *bottleneck* situation[23], enhancing firms' bargaining power vis-à-vis advertisers. A merger also draws focus to total demand, so firms' incentives to differentiate are restored and social welfare increases. The main drawback associated with a merger relates to advertisers, whose surplus is now fully extracted by firms. Our results contrast with those of Anderson et al. (2018), who find that market structure does not affect firms' incentives to differentiate. Conversely, our findings are in line with Steiner (1952), in which differentiation leads to market expansion, and a merger induces firms to focus on total market size.

1.6 Conclusion

107. A vast and long-standing literature has studied product differentiation, particularly in the media industry. However, most existing models assume that consumers single-home. In two-sided environments, consumer multihoming entails platform competition on the advertising side of the market, by raising advertisers' "outside option". In this context, platforms' attention is steered toward demand composition, as opposed to demand size. This scenario is different from standard one-sided environments, where all consumers are equally valuable and firms simply focus on demand size.

23 The platform constitutes the only gateway to consumers for advertisers; thus, the platform holds some monopoly power with respect to advertisers. *Competitive bottleneck* situations are analyzed in Armstrong (2006).

108. We study how firms' incentives to differentiate are affected by consumer multipurchasing (or multihoming) behavior. We identify a new force according to which differentiation may stimulate multipurchasing. If consumers' heterogeneity is weak, then a decrease in characteristic overlap between firms' products leads to more multipurchasing consumers in the market and fewer exclusive consumers. We find that this *overlap-reducing* effect of differentiation leads to market expansion, which results in maximum differentiation in one-sided markets.

109. However, market expansion is an insufficient motivation in two-sided contexts. Our analysis predicts that if platforms do not expect differentiation to lead to market segmentation, minimum differentiation will ensue. This finding can help explain why some advertising-financed markets exhibit a low level of differentiation.

110. We derive interesting implications as regards merger analysis. We show that in multisided environments, a merger is likely to restore platforms' incentives to differentiate. A merger relaxes competition on the advertising market and draws firms' focus to total demand. Our model therefore reconciles theory with empirical contributions that show that ownership concentration leads to greater diversity in media markets. However, in cases where incentives for differentiation are already effective premerger, ownership concentration merely results in lower advertiser surplus. In an era where firms are increasingly able to identify consumers' purchasing behavior, we expect multihoming to play an expanding role in shaping competition between firms relying on advertising revenues or consumer data to generate revenues.

References

Alexandrov, A. (2008). Fat products. *Journal of Economics & Management Strategy*, 17(1), 67-95.

Ambrus, A., Calvano, E., & Reisinger, M. (2016). Either or both competition: A "two-sided" theory of advertising with overlapping viewerships. *American Economic Journal: Microeconomics*, 8(3), 189-222.

Anderson, S. P., Foros, Ø., & Kind, H. J. (2017). Product functionality, competition, and multipurchasing. *International Economic Review*, 58(1), 183-210.

Anderson, S. P., Foros, Ø., & Kind, H. J. (2018). Competition for advertisers and for viewers in media markets. *The Economic Journal*, 128(608), 34-54.

Anderson, S. P., Foros, Ø., & Kind, H. J. (2019). The importance of consumer multihoming (joint-purchases) for market performance: Mergers and entry in media markets. *Journal of Economics & Management Strategy*, 1-13.

Armstrong, M. (2006). Competition in two-sided markets. *The RAND Journal of Economics*, 37(3), 668-691.

Athey, S., Calvano, E., & Gans, J. S. (2016). The impact of consumer multi-homing on advertising markets and media competition. *Management Science*, 64(4), 1574-1590.

Berry, S. T., & Waldfogel, J. (1999). Public radio in the United States: does it correct market failure or cannibalize commercial stations?. *Journal of Public Economics*, 71(2), 189-211.

Berry, S. T., & Waldfogel, J. (2001). Do mergers increase product variety? Evidence from radio broadcasting. *The Quarterly Journal of Economics*, 116(3), 1009-1025

Chen, Y., & Riordan, M. H. (2007). Price and variety in the spokes model. *The Economic Journal*, 117(522), 897-921.

D'Aspremont, C., Gabszewicz, J. J., & Thisse, J. F. (1979). On Hotelling's "Stability in competition". *Econometrica: Journal of the Econometric Society*, 1145-1150.

Fan, Y. (2013). Ownership consolidation and product characteristics: A study of the US daily newspaper market. *American Economic Review*, 103(5), 1598-1628.

Gabszewicz, J. J., Laussel, D., & Sonnac, N. (2001). Press advertising and the ascent of the 'Pensée Unique'. *European Economic Review*, 45(4-6), 641-651.

Gentzkow, M., Shapiro, J. M., & Sinkinson, M. (2014). Competition and ideological diversity: Historical evidence from us newspapers. *American Economic Review*, 104(10), 3073-3114.

George, L. (2007). What's fit to print: The effect of ownership concentration on product variety in daily newspaper markets. *Information Economics and Policy*, 19(3-4), 285-303.

Hotelling, H., (1929). Stability in Competition, *The Economic Journal* 39, 41-57.

Jeziorski, P. (2014). Effects of mergers in two-sided markets: The US radio industry. *American Economic Journal: Microeconomics*, 6(4), 35-73.

Johnson, J. P., & Rhodes, A. (2021). Multiproduct mergers and quality competition. *The RAND Journal of Economics*, 52(3), 633-661.

Kim, H., & Serfes, K. (2006). A location model with preference for variety. *The Journal of Industrial Economics*, 54(4), 569-595.

Lancaster, Kelvin, (1975). Socially Optimal Product Differentiation. *American Economic Review*, vol. 65(4), pages 567-585.

Mullainathan, S., & Shleifer, A. (2005). The market for news. *American Economic Review*, 95(4), 1031-1053.

Salop, S. C. (1979). Monopolistic competition with outside goods. *The Bell Journal of Economics*, 10(1), 141-156.

Spence, M. (1976). Product differentiation and welfare. *The American Economic Review*, 66(2), 407-414.

Spence, M., & Owen, B. (1977). Television programming, monopolistic competition, and welfare. *The Quarterly Journal of Economics*, 103-126.

Steiner, P. O. (1952). Program patterns and preferences, and the workability of competition in radio broadcasting. *The Quarterly Journal of Economics*, 66(2), 194-223.

Sweeting, A. (2010). The effects of mergers on product positioning: evidence from the music radio industry. *The RAND Journal of Economics*, 41(2), 372-397.

APPENDIX

111. We now show how the results we develop in Section 3.2 are affected when we allow for pricing on the consumer side. The profit function of platform i becomes:

$$\pi_i = p_i D_i + rSP_i + \sigma rM\,P.$$

112. The profit function is simply the sum of the profit functions in the one-sided and two-sided cases studied in Sections 3.1 and 3.2. The effects that arise below are therefore a combination of those already identified.

113. ***Prices.*** In the second stage of the game, platform i maximizes its profit function with respect to p_i. The equilibrium price is given by:

$$p_i^* = \frac{1}{4}[\alpha(b-a) + q(2-\alpha) - r(1+\sigma)].$$

114. Equilibrium prices are the same for both firms. Furthermore, the last term in the brackets $r(1+\sigma)$ implies that prices are lower in the two-sided analysis than in the one-sided analysis due to the network effects that consumers exert: an increase in the number of consumers allows the platform to derive more revenue on the advertiser side of the market, which drives consumers' prices down. In this regard, even negative prices could arise provided that r is sufficiently large. However, as in most works considering multisided markets, we restrict the analysis to nonnegative prices. Note that this result motivates our assumption in Section 3.2 that consumers are not charged anything.

115. ***Location choice.*** In the first stage of the game, the platform chooses the location that maximizes its profits, taking into account the optimal price derived in the second stage. The first-order condition is given by:

$$\frac{\partial \Pi}{\partial d} = 0 \Leftrightarrow \frac{\alpha}{4t}[2q - \alpha O] + r\left(1 - \frac{\alpha}{t}\right) + \sigma r\left[\left(\frac{2\alpha}{t} - 1\right) - \frac{\alpha}{2t}\right] = 0.$$

116. The first component is the same as that in the one-sided analysis and is strictly positive (since an increase in differentiation always leads to an increase in total demand), whereas the second and third components can be either positive or negative, as seen in the previous section. The first-order condition can be seen as a combination of the one-sided analysis and two-sided analysis with zero price on the consumer side. Note that the last term $\frac{\alpha}{2t}$ that enters negatively into the third component simply reflects the fact that an increase in differentiation affects prices, which in turn negatively affects the number of multipurchasers in the market.[1] As in Section 3.2, each firm's optimal differentiation strategy is closely related to the value of σ. Proposition 3 is affected in the following way when we allow for consumer pricing in addition to advertising revenues.

117. **Proposition 3':** *In the two-sided setting where firms derive revenue from both consumers and advertising, firms' optimal differentiation strategies are defined as follows:*

- *If revenues from consumers are limited compared to advertising revenues:*
  - *for $\alpha < t$, maximum differentiation arises for every value of σ;*
  - *for $\alpha > t$, there exists a $\bar{\sigma}$ such that maximum differentiation arises provided that $\sigma \geq \bar{\sigma}$, with $\bar{\sigma} < \tilde{\sigma}$, and minimum differentiation arises otherwise.*
- *If revenues from consumers are large compared to advertising revenues: maximum differentiation always arises.*

118. Proposition 3' shows that the general case in which firms derive revenue from both consumers and advertising simply combines elements from Section 3.1 and Section 3.2. On the one hand, firms derive revenue from consumers, which incentivizes them to focus on total demand and hence to increase differentiation. On the other hand, firms derive revenue from advertising, which leads them to also account for the composition of demand and hence to reduce differentiation in those instances mentioned above. If advertising revenues are negligible, firms will focus on total demand, and maximum differentiation will ensue. If advertising revenues are large compared to revenues from consumers, firms may in some instances decide to limit their level of differentiation.

1 Equation (14) shows how the number of multipurchasers in the market is affected by the sum of firms' prices. Conversely, the number of single-purchasers is not affected by prices in equilibrium since both firms' prices affect each firm's exclusive demand in opposite (and proportional) ways, as shown by equations (12) and (13).

119. ***Mergers.*** The analysis of mergers also combines the effects at play in the one-sided and two-sided (with zero price on the consumer side) cases from Section 5. The effect of mergers when platforms derive revenue from consumers and advertising is unambiguous. As seen in Section 3.1, revenues from consumers draw firms' focus to total demand, which results in maximum differentiation. Additionally, a merger strengthens firms' incentives to differentiate, as highlighted in Section 5. Although advertising revenues may refrain platforms from engaging in differentiation (Section 3.2), as discussed above, a merger fully restores platforms' incentives to differentiate. Thus, if platforms derive revenues from both consumers and advertising, a merger will always yield maximum differentiation. The key takeaways derived in Section 5 therefore hold when introducing consumer pricing in addition to advertising revenues.

CHAPTER 2

INFORMATION RETENTION AND OPTIMAL DISCLOSURE RULE

2.1 Introduction

120. In many instances, the economic implications of our choices are surrounded by uncertainty. Fortunately, we can often rely on the advice of more informed parties. A question that has drawn considerable attention in the economic literature is to what extent one can rely on such advice when the more informed party is biased toward one particular outcome. The informed party may decide to reveal only information that is favorable to her cause.

121. The early literature on verifiable disclosure (Grossman, 1981; Milgrom, 1981; Milgrom and Roberts, 1986) argued that such a strategy might not be optimal, for the uninformed party might form pessimistic beliefs about the withheld information. This argument heavily relies on the assumption that communication is costless. If the participation constraint of the informed party is at stake, such a skeptic behavior might not be reasonable. If full information disclosure cannot be achieved through skeptic beliefs, a natural question that arises is whether the uninformed party can use other means to obtain further information.

122. In this paper, we explore the merit of stricter disclosure rules when information is costly to communicate, and this cost is private information. A decision maker consults an adviser before making a binary decision: undertake an action or not. The adviser wishes to persuade the decision maker to undertake the action. The economic consequences of the action can be either positive or negative for the decision maker. The adviser is endowed with N pieces of information that, taken together, are potentially informative about the decision maker's payoff from the action. We take $N = 2$. The adviser can decide whether to send a message and, if so, the amount of information to disclose. Disclosing information may entail a cost to the adviser, which is private information. We ask whether the decision maker would benefit from imposing a minimum amount

of information disclosure or minimum message length, conditional on a message being sent.

123. Several examples can illustrate our setting. An adviser wishes to convince a consumer to have dinner in a particular restaurant. The consumer is unsure about the restaurant's fit with his tastes. The adviser does not know the consumer's tastes but has information about the quality of the two main dishes served at the restaurant (say, meat or fish). Information regarding the quality of each dish can be positive or negative. Thus, the adviser becomes sure of the decision maker's payoff only if she receives two positive or two negative pieces of information, and remains uninformed when receiving conflicting evidence. The adviser can decide to send a message and disclose some or all of his information set through a review platform (e.g., Yelp, TripAdvisor or Google), possibly at a cost. The platform may fear that the adviser discloses only some positive evidence and hence decides whether to impose a minimum review length policy.[1]

124. An alternative interpretation of the model is the following. A prosecutor wants to secure a conviction for a crime and observes two important pieces of information regarding the suspect's implication. The two pieces of information may be indicative of the suspect's guilt, or none of them suggest his involvement. The prosecutor may also observe one evidence pointing to the suspect's implication (say, the murder weapon was found at his place) and another piece of information suggesting the suspect's innocence (say, the suspect has been seen at a public event at the moment of the crime). In this case, the prosecutor remains relatively uninformed about the suspect's guilt. The difference with the previous example is that here, obtaining conflicting evidence is likely coming from a misinterpretation of the information or a weakness in the expertise (the suspect has been framed by someone else or the suspect's alibi was not carefully checked); for if the suspect committed the crime, all the evidence should be consistent with it. Still, the prosecutor may want to disclose only the damning evidence to the jury to obtain the conviction. However, the judge may decide to dismiss the case before trial if the prosecutor fails to show a sufficient amount of concurring evidence against the suspect.[2]

125. The idea that a lack of effort or expertise can lead to a misinterpretation of some pieces of information applies to other situations. An economic expert eager to induce a public policy change may conduct a poor literature review and present only arguments that are seemingly supportive of the policy to the decision maker.

1 Note that as we consider $N = 2$ throughout the paper, a minimum message length policy amounts to a full disclosure requirement.

2 There is an important opportunity cost for the prosecutor in preparing a trial. If the judge assigned to the case has developed a tough reputation in being very demanding (or if the standard of proof has become very demanding), the prosecutor might prefer to reach an agreement with the suspect even if she holds sufficient evidence against him.

To make sure that the expert's recommendation is not based on mixed evidence, the decision maker may decide to implement the policy only if the adviser provides evidence that it will lead to a Pareto improvement of the situation, i.e., that the effect of the policy is unambiguously positive for all the involved parties. This extreme requirement is likely to alleviate the information manipulation problem, but turns out to be very demanding for the adviser.[3] We shall come back on the adviser's incentives to acquire precise information in more depth in the paper.

126. We show that the merit of a demanding disclosure policy hinges on the congruence between the adviser and the decision maker. If the decision maker's initial confidence in the action is high, the policy is inefficient as the adviser can achieve implementation without any communication. The policy is also unlikely to be efficient when the decision maker's initial confidence in the action is sufficiently low. In such a case, the adviser already knows that the only way to convince the decision maker is to provide conclusive evidence in favor of the action. Only for intermediate levels of confidence can the policy increase the decision maker's expected payoff. As we shall see, the decision maker then faces a trade-off between preventing information manipulation and respecting the participation constraint of the adviser.

127. The signal's precision also plays an important role in assessing the effectiveness of the disclosure policy. We show that the effect of the policy is less likely to be positive when the expertise of the adviser is high. In the above example, if the economic expert is known to be very competent, there is no reason to deem the information presented unreliable, as concise as it could be. We also discuss the adviser's incentives to acquire a more precise signal, i.e., to develop expertise. When the signal's precision is endogenous, a stricter disclosure rule is always beneficial. This is because absent the policy, the adviser acquires a signal just precise enough to be able to credibly manipulate the decision maker.

128. **Related literature.** Our paper is primarily related to the classic sender-receiver literature. This literature traditionally differentiates between the transmission of soft information (Crawford and Sobel, 1982) and hard information (Grossman (1981), Grossman and Hart (1980), Milgrom (1981)). As we alluded to above, most of the literature has assumed away any cost of communication. The idea that communication entails cost to the sender/receiver has been analyzed formally more recently.

129. Dewatripont and Tirole (2005) model communication as a moral hazard in teams problem, where both the sender and the receiver must exert costly effort for communication to be successful. They show that the success of

---

3 The assumption here is that the adviser cannot lie, and thus if asked for more information she would have to reveal the negative evidence potentially received regarding the effect of the policy. Of course, asking for more information may also put the expert's participation at risk.

communication hinges on the way information is to be used by the receiver (supervisory vs executive decision making) and the level of congruence between the sender and the receiver. Caillaud and Tirole (2007) consider a sender/multi-receiver setting and study the optimal mechanism for the sender. A receiver can, at a cost, analyze the information provided by the sender. The optimal persuasion strategy involves the sender selectively disclosing information to a subset of receivers to initiate a persuasion cascade. We borrow from these papers the idea that the sender's incentives to transmit information depend on the receiver's initial confidence in the project. In both papers, the information effectively transmitted to the receiver allows him to discover the payoff associated with the action considered. By contrast, we assume that the sender's information structure is composed of several pieces of information that can jointly determine the payoff from the action or not, and that the sender may reveal only some pieces of information. We ask whether the receiver would benefit from imposing more information disclosure in a context of costly communication.

130. A number of papers study the optimal mechanism for the receiver when the amount of information that can be transmitted is limited. In Glazer and Rubinstein (2004), the receiver can only partially verify the sender's message while in Glazer and Rubinstein (2006), the sender can reveal only some of her information. In both papers, the receiver's payoff from the considered action is determined by the joint realization of several aspects (or signals), only observed by the sender. The authors characterize the mechanisms that minimize the probability of a mistake for the receiver. Fishman and Hagerty (1990) study a similar question as we do. They assume that the sender is endowed with N pieces of information but can only reveal one piece, and show that it may be optimal to restrict the set of signals the sender can choose from. A common feature of these papers is that the amount of information that can be transmitted is common knowledge. We assume instead that the cost of communication is private information to the sender and study whether the receiver would benefit from a more demanding disclosure policy. Another way in which we depart from this literature is that in our model, the sender is either perfectly informed or uninformed about the state.[4] This allows us to study the sender's incentives to acquire a more precise signal. We also derive novel results on the interplay between information disclosure rules and the incentives to acquire a more precise signal.

131. The literature on information acquisition has mainly studied the way in which the alignement of the sender and the receiver's preferences or prior views affects the incentives to acquire information (Durr and Swank, 2005; Che and

4 In Glazer and Rubinstein (2004, 2006), the sender knows the state of the world. Fishman and Hagerty (1990) characterize the optimal amount of discretion to allocate to the sender as a function of the signal's (exogenous) precision. They do not discuss the incentives to acquire a more precise signal.

Kartik, 2009). Dewatripont and Tirole (1999) show that hiring several advisers with opposing interests (advocates) results in more efficient information acquisition for the decision maker. In comparison, we focus on the relatively unexplored effect of disclosure rules on a sender's incentives to acquire information.

132. Finally, the paper is related to the recent literature on product discovery. Che and Horner (2018) show that it may be optimal for a welfare maximizing sender to manipulate receivers' beliefs through spamming (i.e., even when the sender does not know the product quality) to foster the discovery of good products. In our setting, even though the sender is biased toward implementation, manipulating the receiver's beliefs can also turn out to be beneficial to the receiver. Importantly, Che and Horner (2018) show that the spamming capacity depends on the signal's precision of the sender. This is also the case in our setting and as we shall see, it plays a key role in driving the sender's incentives to acquire a more precise signal.

133. The rest of the paper is organized as follows. Section 2 presents the model. Section 3 characterizes the adviser's optimal disclosure strategy without any constraint. In Section 4, we analyze the receiver's optimal disclosure policy in the presence of communication costs. In Section 5, we explore the advisor's incentives to acquire more precise information. Section 6 shows that our results are robust when the cost of communication bears on the decision maker. Section 7 concludes.

2.2 The model

134. *a. Actions and payoffs*. There are two parties, the adviser (*A*, she) and the decision maker (*DM*, he). The decision maker has to decide whether to implement an action or stick to the status quo. Implementing the action yields either a gain or a loss to the decision maker. His payoff from the action is given by $u \in \{G, -L\}$, with $G, L > 0$. The realization of u is a priori unknown to the decision maker and his prior that $u = G$ is given by p. However, he may rely on the adviser to obtain information about the payoff associated to the action. The adviser derives a benefit $\beta > 0$ if the action is implemented and is thus interested in inducing the decision maker to undertake it. The status quo yields a payoff 0 to both the decision maker and the adviser.

135. *b. Information structure*. At the outset, the adviser receives a signal σ that is potentially informative of the decision maker's payoff from the action. We assume that the signal consists of two pieces of information that jointly determine the likely payoff of the decision maker. Each piece of information can take one of two values: P (positive) and N (negative). Hence, the adviser can receive three different signals: two positive pieces of information, $\sigma = (P, P)$;

two negative pieces of information, $\sigma = (N, N)$; or one positive and one negative pieces of information, $\sigma = (P, N)$. We assume that the probabilities to observe signal $\sigma \in \{(P, P); (N, N); (P, N)\}$, given the decision maker's payoff, are given by:

$$\Pr[\sigma = (P,P) \mid u] = \begin{cases} \alpha & \text{if} \quad u = G; \\ 0 & \text{if} \quad u = -L, \end{cases}$$

$$\Pr[\sigma = (N,N) \mid u] = \begin{cases} 0 & \text{if} \quad u = G; \\ \alpha & \text{if} \quad u = -L, \end{cases}$$

$$\Pr[\sigma = (P, N) \mid u] = \begin{cases} 1-\alpha & \text{if} \quad u = G; \\ 1-\alpha & \text{if} \quad u = -L. \end{cases}$$

136. This signal's structure implies that the adviser receives a perfectly informative signal with probability α or an uninformative signal with probability $1 - \alpha$.

137. The signal structure we adopt deserves some discussion. First, the idea that an adviser is either fully informed or uninformed about the state of the world has been extensively used in the literature. The assumption that one piece of information can "nullify" another piece of information is also present in Dewatripont and Tirole (1999). In our case, receiving a negative piece of information after receiving a positive one implies that the adviser cannot infer anything about the decision maker's payoff (and is thus informationally equivalent to receiving no news in a more standard setting).[5] Still, a question that remains is why would the adviser receive a signal $\sigma = (P, N)$, i.e., a positive and negative piece of information, if the product is good (or bad) for the decision maker? A first explanation is related to the restaurant example given in the introduction. A product's quality is generally defined across several dimensions, but only a subset of those dimensions may be relevant to the decision maker's payoff. Another potential explanation is that the adviser may sometimes misinterpret a good (resp., bad) information as a bad (resp., good) information. This relates to our economic expert's example. In this case, α may be considered as the level of expertise of the adviser. We shall stick to this last interpretation throughout the paper, as it allows us to conduct a meaningful analysis of the adviser's incentives to acquire more precise information. Broadly speaking, our information structure captures the idea that in the process of collecting evidence in favor of a given project, it is reasonable to assume that the adviser accumulates several pieces of information (instead of the more usual "news or no news" assumption) that may or may not be jointly conclusive about the likely payoff of the project.

5 In some settings, receiving no news conveys some information. This is for instance the case in Dewatripont and Tirole (1999), in which no news is bad news. This is not the case in our setting.

138. *c. Communication strategy*. After observing the signal, the adviser decides whether to disclose information to the decision maker. If she discloses information, she can choose the length of the message, i.e., send one or two pieces of information. We assume that information is hard; the adviser can select what piece of information to send but cannot lie. In what follows, we also assume that the adviser may incur a cost from disclosing information.

139. *d. Timing*. The sequence of events is as follows. First, the adviser receives a signal $\sigma \in \{(P, P), (N, N), (P, N)\}$. Then, the adviser decides whether to send a message m and, if so, the length and content of his message. Finally, the decision maker decides whether to undertake the action or stick to the status quo.

140. The equilibrium concept we rely on is Perfect Bayesian Equilibrium. We restrict our attention to pure strategy equilibria.

2.3 Equilibrium disclosure behavior

141. In this section, we analyze the strategic communication of the adviser as a function of the decision maker's initial confidence in the action, i.e., its prior p. The prior p can also be viewed as a measure of the (ex-ante) alignment of the parties' interests.

142. Suppose first that the sender's strategy consists in disclosing no information, i.e., $m = (\emptyset, \emptyset)$, regardless of the signal received. The decision maker cannot infer anything from this message, so that his posterior remains the same as his prior. In such a case, the decision maker undertakes the action whenever:

$$pG + (1 - p)(-L) > 0 \Leftrightarrow p \geq p_+ = \frac{L}{G + L}. \tag{2.1}$$

143. The decision maker implements the action provided that its prior regarding the action's benefit is large enough. Otherwise, the decision maker sticks to the status quo.

144. Suppose now that the sender's strategy consists in fully revealing the signal obtained. Plainly, the decision maker undertakes the action when the message received is $m = (P, P)$ and sticks to the status quo when receiving $m = (N, N)$, as these messages fully reveal the payoffs from the action. When he receives the message $m = (P, N)$, the posterior of the decision maker is given by:

$$\Pr[u = G | m = (P, N)] = \frac{(1 - \alpha)p}{(1 - \alpha)p + (1 - \alpha)(1 - p)} = p. \tag{2.2}$$

145. As discussed above, the signal (P, N) is completely uninformative and thus, the decision maker undertakes the action when $p > p_+$ and sticks to the status quo otherwise.

146. Let us finally consider the more interesting case where the advisor discloses only one piece of information. Clearly, revealing one negative piece of information would only deteriorate the decision maker's beliefs and does not constitute a sensible candidate strategy for the advisor. Hence, let us focus on the strategy according to which the adviser discloses only one positive piece of information, i.e., $m = (P, \emptyset)$, when obtaining one of the signals $\sigma \in \{(P, P), (P, N)\}$ and discloses no information, i.e., $m = (\emptyset, \emptyset)$ when receiving the signal $\sigma = (N, N)$.[6] The posterior of the decision maker following the message $(P, \emptyset)$ is:

$$\Pr[u = G | m = (P, \emptyset)] = \frac{p}{1 - \alpha(1 - p)} > p. \tag{2.3}$$

147. Sending one positive piece of information rules out the possibility that the signal $\sigma = (N, N)$ was received and thus increases the posterior of the decision maker. This means that the adviser can increase the posterior of the decision maker even when the uninformative signal (P, N) was received. More precisely, the adviser can convince a decision maker with prior belief $p < p_+$ to undertake the action by sending the message $m = (P, \emptyset)$ if:

$$\frac{p}{1 - \alpha(1 - p)} > p_+ \Leftrightarrow p \geq p_- = \frac{p + (1 - \alpha)}{1 - \alpha p_+} \tag{2.4}$$

148. The adviser can convince a skeptic decision maker to undertake the action provided that the decision maker's prior is above the threshold p_-. It is interesting to note that the adviser's ability to manipulate the decision maker's beliefs is closely linked to the precision of her signal. A more precise signal allows the adviser to convince more skeptic decision makers. This happens because, as the precision of the signal improves, a positive piece of information is more likely to stem from the positive signal $\sigma = (P, P)$ than the uninformative signal $\sigma = (P, N)$. We analyze the adviser's incentive to obtain a more precise signal in more depth in Section 5. Proposition 1 below summarizes the above discussion.

149. **Proposition 1.** *There exists an equilibrium in which the amount of information transmitted by the adviser is decreasing in the decision maker's prior:*

- *When $p > p_+$, the adviser does not send any information, regardless of the signal received, and the decision maker undertakes the action;*

---

6 Here, the adviser is indifferent between revealing that the signal $\sigma = (N, N)$ has been received or sending no information, as in both cases the decision maker correctly infers the signal received by the adviser.

- *When $p_- < p < p_+$, the adviser sends (i) a short message $m = (P, \varnothing)$ when he receives a signal $\sigma \in \{(P, P), (P, N)\}$, and the decision maker undertakes the action; (ii) no information when $\sigma = (N, N)$, and the decision maker sticks to the status quo;*
- *When $p < p_-$, the adviser sends (i) a long message $m = (P, P)$ when he receives the signal $\sigma = \{(P, P)\}$, and the decision maker undertakes the action; (ii) no information if $\sigma \in \{(P, P), (P, N)\}$ and the decision maker sticks to status quo.*

150. Although the result that the adviser is less likely to communicate as the initial confidence of the decision maker increases is not surprising, it is interesting to note that, in a model of hard information, the adviser may be able to manipulate the decision maker's beliefs in the absence of conclusive evidence about the state of world. The decision maker's payoff and the adviser's strategy are depicted in Figure 1. In contrast to the adviser, the decision maker's payoff is non-monotonic in his initial confidence about the action.

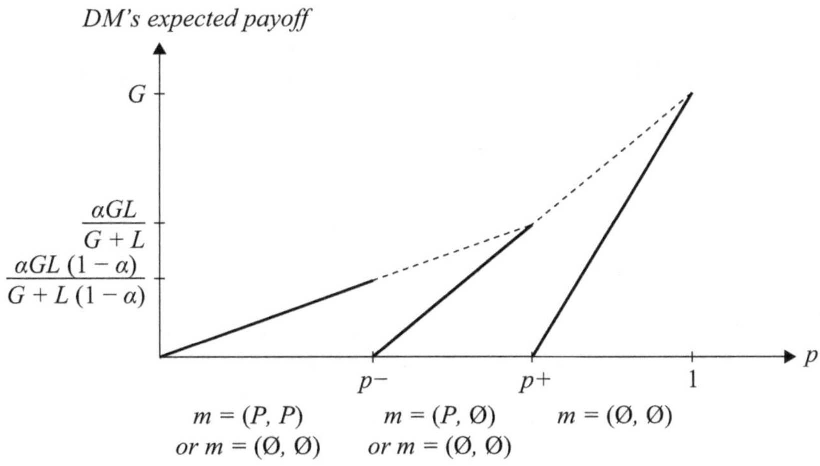

Figure 2.1: Decision maker's expected utility.

151. We note that other equilibria exist. In particular, there exists a fully revealing equilibrium where the adviser perfectly reveals the signal obtained. This equilibrium is supported by pessimistic beliefs from the decision maker. In particular, the decision maker must interpret a message $m = (P, \varnothing)$ as coming from a signal $\sigma = (P, N)$ and a message $m = (\varnothing, \varnothing)$ as coming from a signal $\sigma = (N, N)$. In such a case, the only way for the adviser to convince a skeptic decision maker (i.e., with $p < p_+$) is to disclose the signal $\sigma = (P, P)$. The adviser must also at least disclose the signal $\sigma = (P, N)$ to a confident decision maker (i.e., $p > p+$) to ensure that he implements the action. This equilibrium echoes the standard "unravelling" argument in Milgrom (1981) and Milgrom and Roberts (1986), which involves maximal skepticism from the decision maker.

One reason to believe that the equilibrium described in Proposition 1 is more likely to arise is that, as we elaborate below, communication may be costly.

2.4 Optimal disclosure rule

152. We now consider the possibility for the decision maker to introduce a more demanding disclosure rule, or minimum message length policy. In our setting with two pieces of information, this leaves two options for the adviser: no communication or full information disclosure. In practice, a minimum message length requirement may stem from a third party such as a public authority or a platform. A judge can dismiss a criminal case before trial if the prosecutor fails to show sufficient evidence against the suspect.[7] Several online review platforms also impose similar requirements, either directly or indirectly: TripAdvisor explicitly imposes a minimum message length to leave a review; Google imposes no such requirement explicitly but prominently displays more thorough reviews, which are deemed more relevant. Alternatively, a minimum message length requirement may come directly from the decision maker. A public decision maker may ask for a thorough report to an economic expert on the likely effects of a given policy. During the course of a conversation, the participant who receives an advice may want to sustain the conversation until obtaining sufficient information from the adviser.

153. We also introduce the idea that the adviser may incur a cost to reveal information. In a model of hard information, it is clear that a decision maker would always benefit from more information disclosure if disclosure was costless, as the model confirms in Proposition 2 below. For simplicity, we assume that sending a short message with one piece of information is costless. Sending a second piece of information (i.e., a long message) yields a cost c for the adviser. We assume that c is distributed over $[\underline{c}, \overline{c}]$ with distribution function $F(c)$ and density $f(c)$. We also assume that $\beta \in [\underline{c}, \overline{c}]$.[8]

154. We consider the following modified timing: At $t = 0$, the decision maker decides whether to impose messages with two pieces of information. At $t = 1$, the adviser receives the signal σ and privately observes her cost to disclose information. At $t = 2$, the adviser decides whether to send a message and, if so, the length and content of the message subject to the constraint of the decision

7 In this example, note that the minimum evidence requirement is enforced by a party (the judge) that is different from the decision maker (the jury).

8 If $\beta < \underline{c}$, the decision maker can never obtain a message with two pieces of information and the policy is strictly undesirable. If $\beta > \overline{c}$, the decision maker can always obtain a message with two pieces of information (provided the adviser received conclusive good news) and in such a case, as we show in Proposition 2 below, the policy is always desirable.

maker. At $t = 3$, the adviser decides whether to undertake the action or stick to the status quo.

155. As a benchmark, assume that the cost of sending a long message is zero. We have the following result.

156. **Proposition 2.** *When the cost of sending long messages is zero, imposing long messages benefits the decision maker:*

- *When $p > p_+$, the adviser does not send any information regardless of the signal received and the decision maker undertakes the action;*
- *When $p < p_+$, the adviser sends (i) a long message when he receives the signal $\sigma = \{(P, P)\}$, and the decision maker undertakes the action; (ii) no information if $\sigma \in \{(P, P), (P, N)\}$, and the decision maker sticks to status quo.*
- *A decision maker with prior $p \in (p_-, p_+)$ obtains a strictly higher expected utility from longer messages, while a decision maker with prior $p < p_-$ or $p > p_+$ is not affected by the policy.*

157. As stressed above, it is not surprising that the decision maker benefits from a more demanding disclosure policy in the presence of hard, verifiable information. Still, as Proposition 2 shows, this policy is not strictly beneficial for all types of decision makers. In particular, decision makers with sufficiently large prior beliefs ($p > p_+$) are not affected by the policy, as the adviser can always choose not to send any information. Similarly, a very pessimistic decision maker (with $p < p_-$) does not benefit from the policy. This is because the adviser already needed to send a conclusive message $m = (P, P)$ to convince such a decision maker.

158. Consider now that the adviser incurs a cost c to send a long message. As in the benchmark case, the expected utility of a decision maker with $p < p_-$ or $p > p_+$ does not change with the policy. Let us now focus on the case where $p \in (p_-, p_+)$. The net benefit or loss from imposing longer messages is given by:

$$\begin{aligned} &\int_{\underline{c}}^{\beta} (1-\alpha)\,[(1-p)L - pG]\, dF(c) \\ &- \int_{\beta}^{\bar{c}} (\alpha pG + (1-\alpha)\,[pG + (1-p)(-L)])\, dF(c) \\ &= \underbrace{(1-\alpha)\,[(1-p)L - pG]}_{\text{Benefit } \hat{B}} - \underbrace{\int_{\beta}^{\bar{c}} (\alpha pG)\, dF(c)}_{\text{Loss } \hat{L}} \end{aligned} \tag{2.5}$$

159. Intuitively, the benefit of imposing longer messages is that the adviser can no longer "fool" the decision maker when receiving the signal $\sigma = (P, N)$. Remember that this happens when $p \in (p_-, p_+)$ and that, in such a case, the

expected utility of the decision maker from undertaking the action is negative. On the other hand, the loss from imposing longer messages arises when the adviser's cost of communication is high. In such a case, the adviser does not send any information even when receiving the conclusive signal $\sigma = (P, P)$. The following proposition summarizes the above discussion and performs some comparative statics with respect to the signal's precision α and the sender's benefit β.

160. **Proposition 3.** *When there is a positive cost of sending long messages, imposing long messages has the following effects:*

- *When $p < p_-$ or $p > p_+$, the adviser's strategy and the decision maker's expected payoff are not affected;*
- *When $p_- < p < p_+$, the adviser sends (i) a long message when $\sigma = (P, P)$ and $\beta > c$, and the decision maker undertakes the action; (ii) no message otherwise and the decision maker sticks to the status quo; (iii) the decision maker benefits from the policy if $\hat{B} > \hat{L}$;*
- *The net benefit from the policy is increasing in the sender's payoff β and decreasing in the signal's precision α.*

161. Of particular interest is the result that the likely benefit from the policy is decreasing in the sender's signal precision. A more precise signal makes it increasingly likely that a message $m = (P, \emptyset)$ originates from a signal $\sigma = (P, P)$. In words, if the adviser has a very high level of expertise, the decision maker can safely rely on any piece of information transmitted. In the next section, we explore the adviser's incentives to acquire a precise signal.

2.5 Incentives to acquire a more precise signal

162. A natural issue that arises in our framework relates to the adviser's incentives to acquire information. As we have stressed in previous sections, the signal's precision is key in determining (i) the adviser's ability to manipulate the decision maker's beliefs, and (ii) the likely aggregate effect of a more stringent disclosure policy. This section delivers several new insights regarding the drivers of advisers' incentives to acquire a more precise information.

163. There is an extensive literature studying a sender's incentives to acquire a more precise signal. While it is natural to assume that it is increasingly costly for the sender to acquire precise information, as does most of this literature, we assume away any cost function. As we shall see below, the adviser faces conflicting incentives notwithstanding the absence of any cost. We maintain the assumption

that communication is costly throughout the section, although it is only necessary for Proposition 5. We consider the same timing as in Section 3, except that the adviser first chooses its signal's precision. The following proposition establishes the optimal signal precision from the adviser's point of view.

164. **Proposition 4.** *Suppose that the decision maker's prior is p. The optimal signal precision α^* for the adviser is nonincreasing in p:*

- *(i) if* $p < p_+, \alpha^* = \dfrac{p_+ - p}{p_+(1-p)}$;
- *(ii) if* $p \geq p_+$, $\alpha^* = 0$.

165. The proof is instructive, so we include it below.

166. ***Proof.*** Consider the case where $p < p_+$. We first note that the adviser is strictly worse off choosing a precision level that would result in $p < p_-$. In such a case, the only way for the adviser to convince the decision maker to undertake the action is to receive and reveal the signal $\sigma = (P, P)$. The adviser can do better by choosing α such that $p = p_-$, for in this case, a single positive piece of information is sufficient to convince the decision maker. The adviser is also worse off choosing a precision level that would result in $p > p_-$. To see why this is the case, consider the adviser's ex-ante (expected) payoff when $p_- < p < p_+$: it is equal to $\beta * [\Pr[\sigma = (P, P)] + \Pr[\sigma = (P, N)]] = \beta * [p + (1-p)(1-\alpha)]$. The probability to obtain at least one positive piece of information is decreasing in α, meaning that the adviser benefits from a less precise signal. Hence, the optimal signal precision solves $p = p_- = \dfrac{p_+(1-\alpha^*)}{1-\alpha^* p_+}$ and is given by $\alpha^* = \dfrac{p_+ - p}{p_+(1-p)}$.

167. Consider now the case where $p > p_+$. The decision maker undertakes the action provided that his posterior is larger than p_+. When $\alpha = 0$, the adviser's signal is always uninformative. Hence, the decision maker's decision is based only on its prior. Since $p > p_+$, the decision maker always undertakes the action, and $\alpha = 0$ thus constitutes an optimal strategy for the adviser. ■

168. In fact, when $p \geq p_+$, any precision level leads to the same payoff for the adviser. This is true when we consider, as we do throughout the paper, that the equilibrium in Proposition 1 is the most natural one. Note that if we had considered the fully revealing equilibrium instead, then the adviser would be strictly better off with $\alpha^* = 0$, as in such a case the decision maker has no other choice but to base his decision only on his prior. $\alpha^* = 0$ would also be the unique optimum in the partially revealing equilibrium if we assumed a small cost to acquire information.

169. Proposition 4 states that the adviser does not acquire a more precise signal than what is necessary to credibly manipulate the decision maker. Note that this

result is obtained despite the absence of any cost to acquire information. In standard models of hard information, where the adviser can decide whether to disclose the information obtained or not, the adviser would always prefer a perfectly informative signal if she could obtain it at no cost. A more accurate signal prevents the adviser from manipulating the decision maker in the event that the payoff from the action is bad (i.e., $u = -L$), since obtaining the uninformative signal $\sigma = (P, N)$ becomes less likely. The reason why the adviser is willing to acquire some precision, just enough to convince a decision maker with a prior p, is that otherwise the only way to convince this decision maker is to obtain and communicate the signal $\sigma = (P, P)$.

170. One question that arises is whether this result is just an artefact of the assumption we made regarding the model's information structure, or whether there is an underlying economic meaning behind. We argue that this result helps understand some frequently observed behavior in adviser-decision maker relationships. There is considerable evidence in psychology and the economic applications of psychology of individuals engaging in self-deception strategies to manipulate either their own beliefs or other's beliefs (e.g., Bénabou and Tirole, 2002, 2006). Deciding to remain uninformed or imperfectly informed is a form of self-serving self-deception, for if the adviser knew the truth, she couldn't manipulate the decision maker. Conversely, obtaining apparently mixed evidence or misinterpreting a piece of information allows the adviser to engage in seemingly honest though manipulative communication without engaging her moral conscience. Partisans of a specific candidate for an election rarely check thoroughly information that is presumably beneficial to their cause. A pharmaceutical sales representative may be relatively uninformed about the importance of the side effects of the drug he is trying to promote. Being misinformed constitutes a good excuse, legally or morally, for being wrong ex-post. Developing expertise is costly in that the expert can no longer report misinterpreted or inaccurate information without engaging its good faith.

171. How does a more stringent disclosure policy affect the adviser's incentives? The following proposition discusses the effect of the policy on the adviser's incentives to get a more precise signal and on the decision maker's payoff.[9]

172. **Proposition 5.** *A minimum message length policy affects the adviser's optimal signal precision choice as follows:*

- *(i) if $p < p_+$, the adviser chooses to acquire a perfectly informative signal $\alpha^* = 1$;*

9 The timing we consider here is that of Section 4, except that the sender chooses the signal's precision after observing the decision maker's policy choice.

– *(ii) if $p \geq p_+$, the adviser's signal precision choice is not affected, i.e.,* $\alpha^* = 0$.

The net effect of the policy for the decision maker is strictly positive when $p < p_+$. The policy has no effect when $p \geq p_+$.

173. Unsurprisingly, the policy induces the adviser to acquire the highest possible signal accuracy, provided $p < p_+$. In such a case, the only way to convince the decision maker to implement the action is to receive and transmit the signal $\sigma = (P, P)$. Hence, the adviser wishes to maximize the probability to obtain conclusively good news when the action is beneficial. The effect of the policy is unambiguously positive for the decision maker. Indeed, as discussed above, in the absence of the policy the adviser optimally adjusts the signal precision to the decision maker's prior to make him break even. The decision maker's expected payoff is thus zero in the absence of the policy and becomes positive with the policy.

2.6 Extension: on the decision maker's cost to process information

174. Thus far, we have only considered that communication entails costs for the adviser. In a number of situations though, it is more reasonable to assume that the adviser's participation constraint is satisfied while the decision maker's may be at stake. This is particularly likely when the adviser receives a financial compensation for giving its advice. By contrast, the decision maker may incur either a direct (effort) cost or an opportunity cost to process the information transmitted by the adviser.[10] A public decision maker may order a report to an expert to evaluate the merits of a given policy but may lack the time to carefully read it if the report happens to be too detailed. We argue that, under some mild assumptions, all the results we developed so far remain valid if the cost that arises from communication is borne by the decision maker instead of the adviser.

175. In the same spirit as before, we assume for simplicity that processing a short message (i.e., with one piece of information) is costless for the decision maker but analyzing a long message (i.e., with two pieces of information) generates

10 We do not consider strategies that would involve information overload by the adviser. This type of strategy would only be interesting to consider for the adviser in the case where $p > p_+$, to induce the decision maker to "rubber-stamp" the action/project, i.e., implement it without analyzing the message received. However, in the equilibrium we consider throughout the paper, the adviser can do equally well by not sending any information. This strategy would be more interesting to consider in the fully revealing equilibrium described in Section 3.

a cost c. The cost c is distributed over $[\underline{c}, \overline{c}]$ with distribution function $F(c)$ and density $f(c)$. We also assume $\underline{c} < G < \overline{c}$. The most important assumption we rely on is the following. The cost that the decision maker has to incur to process a long message is private information of the adviser, and the decision maker discovers this cost only when he is faced with a long message. There are plenty of situations where a principal has better information on the task to be performed by an agent. In the example given above, the expert may want to send a concise report because she knows that the decision maker will not have the time or ability to analyze a detailed and technical report. A professor may decide to omit a proof because she knows it would be too costly for the students to understand it.

176. Proposition 1 and 2 do not rely on any cost and are thus not affected. As to the effect of a minimum message length policy on the decision maker's payoff, equation (5) above simply becomes:

$$\underbrace{(1-\alpha)[(1-p)L-pG]}_{\text{Bebefit } \tilde{B}} - \underbrace{\int_{G}^{\overline{c}} (\alpha pG)\, dF(c).}_{\text{Loss } \tilde{L}} \tag{2.6}$$

177. It is clear that the main trade-off for the policy is not affected when we consider that the cost of communication is borne by the decision maker.

178. **Proposition 6.** *When there is a positive cost to process long messages and the signal's precision is exogenous, imposing long messages yields the following effects:*

- *When $p < p_-$ or $p > p_+$, the adviser's strategy and the decision maker's expected payoff are not affected;*
- *When $p_- < p < p_+$, the adviser sends (i) a long message when $\sigma = (P, P)$ and $G > c$, and the decision maker undertakes the action; (ii) no message otherwise and the decision maker sticks to status quo; (iii) the decision maker benefits from the policy if $\tilde{B} > \tilde{L}$;*
- *The net benefit from the policy is decreasing in the signal's precision α.*

Proposition 1, 2, 4 and 5 are not affected.

2.7 Conclusion

179. This paper has explored the merit of demanding disclosure rules in a context where communication might be costly and this cost is private information to the adviser. Our study delivers several takeaways.

180. First, it shows that the benefit from a minimum message length policy is non-monotonic in the decision maker's initial confidence in the project. Extreme skepticism prevents any form of information manipulation, while excessive optimism hurts the decision maker if the adviser's participation cannot be imposed. Still, if the decision maker's level of confidence leaves room for information manipulation by the adviser, a more demanding disclosure policy might be beneficial. The optimal disclosure policy then trades-off the suppression of information manipulation with the adviser's participation constraint.

181. Second, the adviser's ability to manipulate the decision maker is determined by her level of expertise. The decision maker is more easily manipulated when the adviser's expertise is high. Still, a competent adviser is often well informed and thus a more demanding disclosure policy is less desirable in this context. This is particularly likely to be true if the adviser's expertise and her opportunity cost of communication are positively correlated, as one may expect. When the level of expertise is endogenous, the adviser provides just the sufficient level of effort to credibly manipulate the decision maker. In this case, being more demanding is desirable for the decision maker.

182. The paper emphasizes the adviser's cost of communication. However, as we have seen, the model readily applies to situations in which the cost of communication is borne by the decision maker, to the extent that the adviser is better informed about this cost than the decision maker.

183. Our work leaves many questions open. We have assumed throughout the paper that information is hard, verifiable. However, one may wonder about the effect of stricter disclosure rules when the adviser has the possibility to lie, i.e., when information is soft. There may be an interesting link between the length of a message and the nature of information. If lying is costly, and this cost increases with the message length, then longer messages are more likely to be reliable (the information transmitted becomes "harder"). An efficient disclosure policy must then, as in our work, trade-off a more informative message with the adviser's participation constraint. Another interesting research question would be to consider how the presence of multiple decision makers with different prior beliefs affects the desirability of a demanding disclosure policy. In particular, when choosing the precision of her signal, the adviser must balance the positive effect of being able to convince more decision makers with the negative effect of obtaining more often conclusively bad news (and thus not being able to manipulate the decision maker). In the context of multiple decision makers with different priors, the expected payoff of each decision maker will be different for a given level of signal precision, and they may thus disagree regarding the merit of a more demanding disclosure policy. These questions are left for future research.

References

Bénabou, R., & Tirole, J. (2002). Self-confidence and personal motivation. *The Quarterly Journal of Economics*, 117(3), 871-915.

Bénabou, R., & Tirole, J. (2006). Belief in a just world and redistributive politics. *The Quarterly Journal of Economics*, 121(2), 699-746.

Caillaud, B., & Tirole, J. (2007). Consensus building: How to persuade a group. *American Economic Review*, 97(5), 1877-1900.

Che, Y. K., & Hörner, J. (2018). Recommender systems as mechanisms for social learning. *The Quarterly Journal of Economics*, 133(2), 871-925.

Che, Y. K., & Kartik, N. (2009). Opinions as incentives. *Journal of Political Economy*, 117(5), 815-860.

Crawford, V. P., & Sobel, J. (1982). Strategic information transmission. *Econometrica: Journal of the Econometric Society*, 1431-1451.

Dewatripont, M., & Tirole, J. (1999). Advocates. *Journal of Political Economy*, 107(1), 1-39.

Dewatripont, M., & Tirole, J. (2005). Modes of communication. *Journal of Political Economy*, 113(6), 1217-1238.

Dur, R., & Swank, O. H. (2005). Producing and manipulating information. *The Economic Journal*, 115(500), 185-199.

Fishman, M. J., & Hagerty, K. M. (1990). The optimal amount of discretion to allow in disclosure. *The Quarterly Journal of Economics*, 105(2), 427-444.

Glazer, J., & Rubinstein, A. (2004). On optimal rules of persuasion. *Econometrica*, 72(6), 1715-1736.

Grossman, S. J. (1981). The informational role of warranties and private disclosure about product quality. *The Journal of Law and Economics*, 24(3), 461-483.

Grossman, S. J., & Hart, O. D. (1980). Disclosure laws and takeover bids. *The Journal of Finance*, 35(2), 323-334.

Milgrom, P. R. (1981). Good news and bad news: Representation theorems and applications. *The Bell Journal of Economics*, 380-391.

Milgrom, P., & Roberts, J. (1986). Relying on the information of interested parties. *The RAND Journal of Economics*, 18-32.

Sobel, J. (2013). Giving and receiving advice. *Advances in economics and econometrics*, 1, 305-341.

Szalay, D. (2005). The economics of clear advice and extreme options. *The Review of Economic Studies*, 72(4), 1173-1198.

CHAPTER 3

ENTRY AND UPSTREAM COMPETITION IN THE CHILEAN TELECOMMUNICATIONS MARKET[1]

3.1 Introduction

184. In many markets, competition takes place between integrated firms and independent retailers. A typical example is offered by the oil market, in which the main oil refiners usually compete with independent firms (e.g., hypermarkets/ big box stores) at the retail level. Similarly, Microsoft operates the most widely used operating system and competes with several manufacturers in the market for laptops or tablets. In network industries, this type of market structure is extensively observed. In telecommunication markets, in particular, mobile network operators (MNOs) face competition from virtual mobile network operators (MVNOs), which purchase access to their network infrastructure to compete in the retail market.

185. A salient issue is to determine what drives the incentives of integrated firms to provide access to a downstream competitor. Intuitively, the higher the market share of the independent firm in the downstream market, the higher the incentives of the integrated firms to provide access.[2] Intense upstream competition may thus ensue to offer access to the independent firm. Another important issue is to determine how providing access to a competitor affects downstream competition, and more particularly, the pricing strategy of the access provider. Surprisingly, few empirical literature explore the incentives of integrated incumbents to provide access to an essential input and the interplay between access provision and downstream competition.

1 This paper was written with Vicente Lagos (Telecom Paris, Institut Polytechnique de Paris).

2 We abstract from any anti-competitive behavior, whereby integrated firms would try to exclude an independent retailer from the market.

186. We analyze the Chilean mobile telecommunications market, where a new operator, WOM, entered the market in June 2015. Before entry, three mobile network operators operated in the market: Entel (the historical operator and market leader), Movistar (second oldest operator), and Claro (third entrant). These three incumbent MNOs essentially relied on their own network to provide services to consumers. The entry of WOM had a huge impact on the market: prices fell and incumbents' market shares were dramatically affected.

187. Upon entering the market, WOM had to rely on network access contracts (roaming) to provide sufficient quality (mobile coverage) to consumers. Indeed, although WOM held spectrum licenses when it entered the market, rolling out a mobile network is expensive and can take several years. Thus, WOM initially relied on a national roaming contract with Entel, giving it Entel's infrastructure. However, after several failed attempts to renegotiate the terms of the contract with Entel, WOM switched to Movistar in May 2017.[3] Entel and Movistar were the two incumbent MNOs operators most affected by entry. We posit that WOM's disproportionate cannibalization of Entel and Movistar's market shares entailed intense wholesale competition between the two operators to provide access. Indeed, providing access allows an operator to (partially) recoup downstream profit losses through access revenues.

188. We further investigate how access provision affects an incumbent's pricing strategy in the downstream market. Since downstream profit losses are partially recouped through access revenues, the access provider may have limited incentives to reduce its downstream prices upon entry. Indeed, although the financial terms of access contracts are usually secrets, it is well known that access revenues can reach considerable amounts.[4]

189. To explore these issues, we build a dataset on the Chilean mobile telecommunications market in the period 2013-2022. This period covers both entry (June 2015) and the switch of access provider (May 2017). We develop a supply model where the access provider sets the wholesale price first and then competition takes place in the downstream market. We estimate a structural demand model to derive consumers' substitution patterns and combine these estimates with the supply model to recover firms' wholesale and retail margins. We examine whether the decrease of Entel's retail prices that occurred around

3 La Tercera (May 2017): "Market sources indicate that WOM signed with Movistar in order to terminate the network contract that it currently has with Entel… This, since the prices of Entel's roaming contracts are known to be considerably higher than the offer of the other operators." https://www.latercera.com/noticia/wom-suma-proveedor-movistar-opera-las-tres-grandes/

4 In France, the mobile telecommunications market experienced a similar pattern than in Chile. In 2012, a fourth MNO, "Free", entered with an aggressive pricing strategy. Free signed a roaming contract to access Orange's network, the historical operator. Pierre Louette, one of Orange's top officials, declared: "We were convinced to lose money on the retail market because of Free Mobile; these roaming revenues act as a waterbed. We are already going to earn more than a billion euros in two years, that's beyond our hopes… This contract almost covers our yearly mobile network investments." https://www.challenges.fr/high-tech/le-contrat-d-itinerance-avec-free-fait-la-fortune-d-orange_120

June 2017 can be rationalized by the loss of the access contract. We argue that the loss of the access contract likely increased the relative importance of retail revenues for Entel, who could not afford losing more market shares.

190. **Related literature.** Our analysis builds on theoretical contributions studying entry in vertically integrated markets. There is a long-standing literature examining vertical integration and foreclosure (Salinger (1988); Hart and Tirole (1990); Ordover, Saloner and Salop (1990)). We do not consider foreclosure issues and focus instead on the interplay between downstream and upstream competition. Ordover and Shaffer (2007) study a scenario with two integrated incumbents and one potential entrant which sell differentiated products downstream. The authors show that if the entrant captures market shares from both incumbents, intense upstream competition will arise. Bourreau, Hombert, Pouyet and Schutz (2011) study a similar setting and show that the incumbent that provides access has incentives to increase its retail price, which can relax downstream and upstream competition. The mechanism at play is akin to the upward pricing pressure index frequently used in merger analysis, whereby the merging firms increase their prices anticipating that some sales will divert to each other.

191. In the current setting, the rationale is similar: when the entrant enters the market, the sales that she cannibalizes from the access provider are not totally lost, as access provider derives access revenues from them. In line with these theoretical predictions, we study how the evolution of cannibalization by the entrant over time shapes competition in the upstream market, and how providing access to the entrant affects the retail price set by the access provider.

192. On the empirical side, we contribute to the literature examining the effect of entry on an incumbent's behavior. Goolsbee and Syverson (2008) show that the mere threat of entry triggers price cuts by incumbent firms in the airline industry. In the telecommunications industry, Seim and Viard (2011) find that entry led incumbents to offer both lower prices and greater variety. Nicolle, Grzybowski and Zulehner (2018) examine the impact of Free Mobile's entry in the French market using hedonic price regressions and report significant drops in prices. Bourreau, Sun and Verboven (2021) also study the impact of Free Mobile's entry. They discuss the simultaneous introduction of fighting brands by incumbents and show that this decision can be rationalized as a breakdown of tacit collusion on product offerings due to entry. We study the Chilean telecommunication market and show that the impact of entry on retail prices may be smaller for an integrated incumbent that provides access to the entrant.

193. Our work also is also related to the literature on mergers. Miller and Weinberg (2017) analyze a merger in the brewing industry using a structural model of

demand and supply and find that the magnitude of the price increase that followed the merger cannot be rationalized by a change in Nash-Bertrand equilibrium. They suggest that the merger may have facilitated price coordination in the market. Björnerstedt and Verboven (2014) perform an ex-post merger simulation in the Swedish analgesics market and discuss how well merger simulations can predict changes in market outcomes. Their work contributes more broadly to the enduring debate on the reliability of structural econometric models to predict counterfactual outcomes, as exemplified by the disagreement between Angrist and Pischke (2010) and Nevo and Whinston (2010). We show that changes in vertical relationships entail similar effects than mergers in markets with integrated firms using counterfactual simulations from a structural model.

194. Finally, our research contributes to the literature on vertical relations, and more particularly on vertical integration and competition. Hastings (2004) analyzes the US gasoline market and shows that vertical integration leads to higher prices. Closer to our paper, Luco and Marshall (2020) study the effects of vertical integration by multiproduct firms. They find that although vertical integration eliminates double-marginalization, which tends to affect prices negatively, it also induces the multiproduct firm to increase the price of its other products so as to divert sales towards its "integrated" product. This *Edgeworth-Salinger effect* arises because integration makes one product relatively more profitable to sell. Our mechanism does not rely on an increase in retail margins. Nevertheless, we show that the operator that provides access to the entrant reacts less aggressively to entry, since all the retail sales lost to the entrant generate wholesale profits.

195. The paper is organized as follows. In Section 2, we provide a description of the industry, the data and the main effects of entry on prices and market shares. In Section 3, we introduce the model of demand and supply. We present our results in Section 4. Section 5 concludes.

3.2 The market and the effects of entry

196. In this section, we provide a description of the industry and the data. We also analyze the effects of entry on firms' prices and market shares. This analysis motivates our subsequent structural analysis in Sections 3 and 4.

3.2.1 The market for mobile telecommunications in Chile

197. The Chilean telecommunication market is a particularly dynamic and competitive market. The historical operator, Entel, was privatized in 1992 and competition was rapidly introduced in the market. Early privatization

allowed for the development of several firms which currently compete in the mobile telecommunications market. Until 2015, the market for mobile services was operated by three mobile network operators (MNOs): Entel, Movistar, and Claro. In 2015, a new MNO entered the market, WOM, which dramatically affected the incumbent MNOs. Upon entry, WOM relied on a national roaming contract to be able to provide sufficient coverage to consumers.

198. National roaming happens when a company can access an incumbent's mobile network for the whole country, allowing the access seeker to offer services on a national basis. Such agreements can be concluded between a mobile network operator and a mobile virtual network operator (MVNO). MVNOs are operators that do not own a mobile network and must rely on MNOs to provide mobile services. Entrant MNOs may also sign national roaming agreements to be able to provide full geographic coverage from the beginning, while progressively rolling out their own network. In some countries, national roaming is imposed by national regulation agencies (NRAs) in the terms of spectrum licenses to facilitate entry and stimulate competition in the market. In other instances, national roaming agreements can be implemented for commercial purposes without the request from the NRA.[5]

199. In Chile, national roaming agreements are provided on a voluntary basis by MNOs, for commercial purposes. Upon entering the market in June 2015, WOM signed a national roaming contract with Entel, which is perceived as the highest quality operator in the market. While the exact terms of national roaming contracts are usually kept secret, it is well-known that they can reach considerable amounts. These contracts may thus have an important impact on the market, affecting the cost and thus the price of the entrant, but also the price of the network-access provider, as we elaborate below. The roaming contract was initially signed for a period of two years, until May 2017. At the beginning of 2017, tensions arose between WOM and Entel upon contract renewal. Market sources indicate that Entel's roaming prices were high, and that WOM tried to negotiate lower access charges. At the same time, Movistar started discussing with WOM to become its new access provider. Renegotiations with Entel eventually failed and WOM switched to Movistar as a new access provider in May 2017.

3.2.2 Dataset

200. Our first dataset comes from the Chilean telecommunications regulator (Subtel). For each month during the period October 2017-June 2022, we observe all the plans available for each of the four mobile network operators and the number

5 For example, in France, 2G national roaming is enforced by the regulator, while 3G agreements are based on commercial arrangements between operators. For an overview of national roaming regulations in many countries, see the National Roaming for Resilience report by the European Union Agency for Network and Information Security.

of consumers associated to each plan. This dataset also includes information about data and call allowances for each plan. The data also comprises information about plans launched before October 2017 that still exhibit a positive number of consumers in the period of observation. This allows us to estimate substitution patterns between plans launched shortly before October 2017 and after this date.

201. Our second dataset was collected manually from the Internet Archive (Wayback Machine). For each month during the period January 2013-June 2022, we collected information on every postpaid plan[6] and its associated characteristics for the four mobile network operators. For each plan, we observe the main characteristics: price, call and data allowances. The combination of these two datasets gives us a clear picture of the evolution of firms' offerings over time, and our observation period covers both entry (in June 2015) and the change of roaming provider (in May 2017). The final dataset consists in 3,419 observations, corresponding to hundreds of different plans, with most of the plans being available over several months. There are on average 8 plans per firm in a month.[7] Table 1 below presents summary statistics for the main variables, broken down by operators. Entel is perceived as the highest network quality firm in the market, before Movistar and Claro. As shown in Table 1, this is reflected in its price, which is generally higher than competitors.[8] This higher price is also generally associated to higher data and call allowances. In comparison, the price of WOM is particularly low, in line with its aggressive strategy.

202. Since we do not observe plan-level market shares before October 2017, the structural analysis conducted in Sections 3 and 4 is limited to the effect of the change in roaming provider on Entel's prices. However, the data allows us to study the effect of entry on firms' prices. We also obtain data on firms' aggregate market shares at the month level on the postpaid market (corresponding essentially to plans with both call and data allowances), which allows us to study the effect of entry on market shares. We analyze the effects of entry in the next subsection.

Firm	Variable	Mean	SD	Min	Max
Entel	Price	29.99	15.99	6.99	69.99
	Data allowance (GB)	36.74	68.84	0.2	420
	Call allowance (min)	1673.2	1279.67	70	3000

6 We consider plans that include both call and data allowances.

7 The number of different plans offered by firms tends to decrease over time.

8 Prices are given in dollars.

Firm	Variable	Mean	SD	Min	Max
Movistar	Price	28.20	15.25	7.99	72.98
	Data allowance (GB)	30.05	60.33	0.25	360
	Call allowance (min)	1415.97	1224.63	70	3000
Claro	Price	26.98	15.76	6.9	89.99
	Data allowance (GB)	23.66	39.31	0.1	153.6
	Call allowance (min)	1667.86	1273.55	55	3000
WOM	Price	17.13	6.68	7.99	29.99
	Data allowance (GB)	30.34	32.76	1.5	300
	Call allowance (min)	1526.28	1189.59	100	3000

Table 3.1: Main market characteristics.

3.2.3 The effect of entry on prices and market shares

203. We now turn to the analysis of the effects of entry on firms' prices and on market shares. As discussed above, WOM entered the market with an aggressive pricing strategy, which triggered different price responses by incumbents. Market shares were affected accordingly.

204. ***Price effects.*** To shed light on the evolution of prices following WOM's entry, we follow the approach of Björnerstedt and Verboven (2016) and estimate the following regression:

$$\ln p_{it} = \alpha + \beta PostEntry_t \times Treated_i + \gamma X_{it} + \epsilon_{it}, \tag{3.1}$$

where p_{it} represents the price of plan i, X_{it} is a vector of plan characteristics, $PostEntry_t$ is a dummy variable equal to 1 after WOM enters the market, and $Treated_i$ is a dummy variable equal to 1 if the plan is offered by Movistar or Claro.[9] This equation is similar to a standard difference-in-difference regression. The underlying idea is that Entel's prices have not been much affected by WOM's entry, in comparison with Movistar and Claro. As underlined by Björnerstedt and Verboven (2016), in merger analysis, it is often assumed that the merger has no effect on the prices of firms that are not part of the merger. While the current situation is different than a merger, it entails similar effects than in merger analysis. Providing access to the entrant reduces incentives to decrease retail prices upon entry, since the access provider faces an opportunity cost, in terms of lost access revenues. We may thus expect Entel's prices to remain relatively high after entry. By contrast, downstream sales represent the

9 There are other ways to estimate the evolution of quality-adjusted prices over time. For instance, Nicolle, Grzybowski and Zulehner (2018) perform hedonic price regressions and analyze the evolution of time fixed-effect coefficients. We conducted a similar analysis and found results consistent with the present findings. This analysis is reported in the Appendix.

only source of profits for the other incumbents, Movistar and Claro. These firms are more likely to decrease their prices following entry, to avoid losing too much market shares. Hence, in integrated markets, entry can have heterogeneous effects on firms' prices.

205. In addition to the previous regression, we estimate the impact of entry on prices for each firm in isolation:

$$\ln p_{ijt} = \alpha_j + \beta_j PostEntry_t + \gamma_j X_{ijt} + \epsilon_{ijt}, \tag{3.2}$$

where p_{ijt} is the price of plan i sold by firm j. The results of regressions (1) and (2) are reported in Table 2 below. In particular, we use two different time windows to assess the robustness of our results: a one-year time window (i.e., 6 months before and after entry), and a two-year time window (i.e., 1 year before and after entry).

	Price						Market share 2.5 year window Percent point change
	1-year window			2-year window			
	Coefficient	Percent	change	Coefficient	Percent	change	
Difference-in-difference							
PostEntry × Treated	−.1319*** (.0227)		−12.36	−.2144*** (.0156)		−19.29	
R^2		0.855			0.8412		
Regression firm-level							
Entel: Entry	−.0593 (.0359)		0	−.0624*** (.0243)		−6.05	−3.94*** (.47)
Movistar: Entry	−.0608** (.0243)		−5.9	−.1085*** (.0176)		−10.28	−1.17*** (.31)
Claro: Entry	−.2291*** (.0409)		−20.48	−.3038*** (0.029)		−26.20	−1.26*** (0.2)

We take $(\exp(\beta) - 1) * 100$ to obtain percent changes in prices from coefficients. Robust standard errors are reported in parentheses.

* $p < 0.1$, ** $p < 0.05$, *** $p < 0.01$

Table 3.2: Effect of entry on prices and market shares.

206. Our results are broadly consistent with our expectations. Our "difference-in-difference" estimator shows that Movistar and Claro's prices have experienced a 12.36 percentage reduction relative to Entel's prices within a few months after entry. Our two-year time window shows a larger effect of 19.29 percentage reduction. Our regressions at the firm level provide further details about the decomposition of these effects. In the 1-year time window, our estimates reveal no significant price decrease by Entel. In comparison, Movistar and Claro's

prices have decreased by 6 and 20 percent, respectively, within the same time frame. Claro's important price reduction might be explained by its low-cost positionning in the market, making it a close substitute to WOM's low-cost offer. In the two-year time window, we observe a significant 6 percent reduction in Entel's price, still much below Movistar and Claro's 10 and 26 percent price reductions. These price reductions are mainly due to increase in data and call allowances. These results seem to confirm that Entel had weaker incentives to decrease prices than the other incumbents, Movistar and Claro, when WOM entered the market. In Section 4, we provide a detailed analysis of Entel's prices in the period that followed the switch of network access provider. We show that Entel's incentives were significantly affected when WOM switched to Movistar.

207. *Market share effects.* We have seen that WOM's entry triggered different price responses by the incumbents. A follow-up question is whether these different responses also led to different market shares impact on the incumbents. To investigate this question, we conducted regressions similar to (2), i.e., we estimate the impact of entry on firms' market shares. One important caveat here is that we only observe market shares at the aggregate level (month) for the period around entry. We thus use a different, larger time frame to capture the main market share effects that followed entry. The time window we consider begins six month before the entry of WOM and extends to two years after. Hence, this time frame captures the period where tensions started to arise in the upstream market. In particular, we argue that Movistar started to lose substantial market share at the end of 2016, which may explain why it was willing to provide access to WOM.

208. Our estimates (reported in Table 2) show that Entel's market share declined by a substantial 4 percentage points after entry. This is consistent with the fact that Entel did not decrease prices by much following entry; and that he could afford losing some market shares while providing network access to the entrant. Our results also reveal that the impact of entry was more limited for Movistar and Claro, which both experienced a 1.2 percentage point drop in market shares after entry. However, while the impact of entry on Claro's market share is stable over time, Movistar seemed to experience a more subtle pattern. Figure 2 below shows the evolution of firms' market shares. While Movistar's market share appears to be relatively stable in the year following entry, it seems to experience a strong decline in its market share around mid-2016. Interestingly, this decline is relatively similar to the one experienced by Entel at the end of 2016 and beginning of 2017. WOM's disproportionate cannibalization of Entel and Movistar's market shares might thus be one potential reason for the wholesale competition that ensued in 2017.

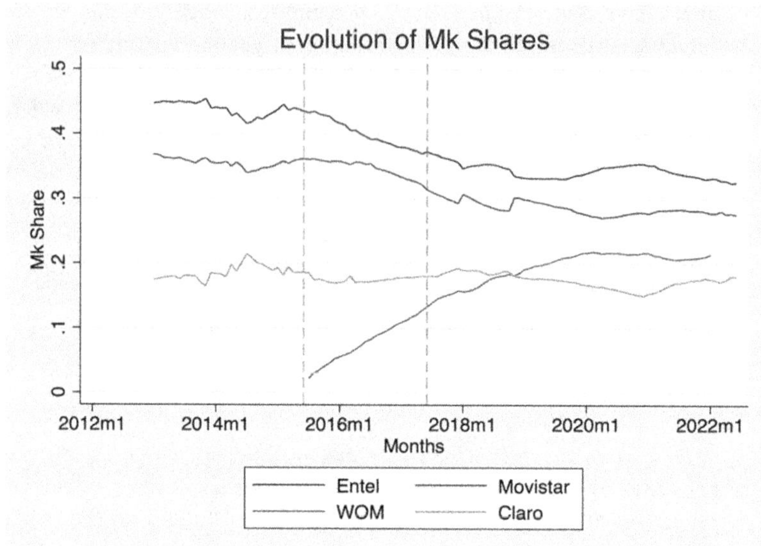

Figure 3.1: Evolution of market shares.

3.3 Model

209. In this section, we build a structural model of demand and supply to analyze the sudden price drop of Entel that followed WOM's switch of network access provider. We show that this price drop can be rationalized by our structural model.

3.3.1 Demand

210. We use a nested logit model to represent consumers' demand. Although this modelling assumption puts some restrictions on consumers' substitution patterns, it allows to derive simple closed-form formulas for firms' estimated market shares.[10] The nested logit model partitions the set of alternatives faced by a consumer into subsets, called nests. For two alternatives that belong to the same nest, the ratio of probabilities[11] is independent of the attributes of other alternatives (the independance of irrelevant alternatives, or IIA assumption, holds within each nest). This means that alternatives that belong to the same nest exhibit the same cross-price elasticities. Conversely, for alternatives that belong to different nests, the ratio of probabilities can depend on the attributes

10 We are currently working on the estimation of a random coefficient logit model (following Berry, Levinsohn and Pakes, 1995), which allows for richer substitution patterns.

11 In discrete choice models such as logit, nested logit and random coefficient logit, the probability of choosing a given product is used to represent market share.

of other alternatives in the two nests (the cross-price elasticities between different nests are different than the within-nest cross-price elasticities). The utility that consumer *i* obtains from purchasing product *j* at date *t* is as follows:

$$U_{ijt} = \beta x_{jt} - \alpha p_{jt} + \xi_{jt} + (1 - \sigma)\epsilon_{ijt} + \zeta_{igt},$$

where p_{jt} represents the price of the product, x_{jt} is a vector of observed characteristics and ξ_{jt} is a vector of unobserved product characteristics. The term $(1 - \sigma)\epsilon_{ijt}$ represents the unobserved random error and is assumed to follow a type I extreme value distribution. Finally, ζ_{igt} is a term that is common to all products in nest *g*; it represents the deviation from the mean random error. The parameter $\sigma \in [0, 1]$ captures the correlation of consumer preferences within a nest.

3.3.2 Supply model

211. There are four mobile network operators (MNOs) in the Chilean telecommunications market: Entel (*E*), Movistar (*M*), Claro (*C*) and WOM (*W*). While the incumbent MNOs rely on their own network to offer services, the entrant WOM owns a very limited network and needs to purchase wholesale access from one of the incumbents to provide sufficient coverage to its customers.

212. We consider the following two-stage game. In the first stage, the access provider sets its wholesale price. In the second stage of the game, the four MNOs set their retail prices for consumers given the observed wholesale price. This model entails the traditional double-marginalization outcome. Finally, to keep the exposition simple, we present the model assuming that each MNO is a single-product firm.[12]

213. Let $A = \{E, M, C, W\}$ be the set of all MNOs and $B = \{E, M, C\}$ the subset of incumbent MNOs. We denote by *b* the incumbent MNO who provides access to the entrant. The profit of an incumbent $i \in B$ is given by:

$$\pi_i = (p_i - c_i)D_i(\boldsymbol{p}) + I_{i=b}(w_w - c_w)D_w(\boldsymbol{p}), \tag{3.3}$$

where $I_{i=b}$ is an indicator function that takes value 1 if the incumbent MNO *i* is the access provider and 0 otherwise; w_w is the wholesale price charged to the entrant WOM; c_w is the marginal cost of providing access; c_i is the marginal cost of product *i*; and $D_i(\boldsymbol{p})$ and $D_w(\boldsymbol{p})$ represent the demand for product *i* and *w*, respectively. The profit of the entrant is simply:

$$\pi_w = (p_w - w_w)D_w(\boldsymbol{p}). \tag{3.4}$$

12 The extension to multiproduct firms is straightforward but at the cost of additional notational burden. Note that the model can also be extended to several wholesale suppliers. See Villas-Boas (2007) for a general treatment and Bourreau, Sun and Verboven (2021) for an application to the mobile telecommunications sector.

214. Note that the entrant's marginal cost is normalized to zero. As shown by Bourreau, Sun and Verboven (2021), it can be considered as implicitly included in the access provider's marginal cost to provide access c_w, and hence, in the wholesale price w_w.

215. We solve this game following the original work of Villas-Boas (2007) and more particularly Bourreau, Sun and Verboven (2021). First, we derive the optimal retail prices for a given wholesale price. Then, we proceed with the first stage of the game and derive the optimal condition for the wholesale price. Combining these conditions allows us to retrieve retail and wholesale margins.

216. In the second stage, the first order conditions for retail profit maximization are given by:

$$\frac{\partial \pi_i}{\partial p_i} = D_i + (p_i - c_i)\frac{\partial D_i}{\partial p_i} + \mathrm{I}_{i=b}(w_w - c_w)\frac{\partial D_w}{\partial p_i} = 0, \tag{3.5}$$

$$\frac{\partial \pi_w}{\partial p_w} = D_w + (p_w - w_w)\frac{\partial D_w}{\partial p_w} = 0. \tag{3.6}$$

217. These equations implicitly define retail prices as functions of the wholesale price. Given these retail prices, the access provider maximizes its profit function $\pi_b = (p_b(w_w) - c_b)D_b(\boldsymbol{p}(w_w)) + (w_w - c_w)D_w(\boldsymbol{p}(w_w))$ with respect to w_w. The first order condition is given by:

$$\frac{d\pi_b}{dw_w} = \frac{\partial \pi_b}{\partial w_w} + \sum_{j \in A} \frac{\partial \pi_b}{\partial p_j}\frac{\partial p_j}{\partial w_w}.$$

218. An increase in w_w implies both a direct effect on the access provider's profit and indirect effects through its impact on retail prices. Applying the envelope theorem and substituting for $\frac{\partial \pi_b}{\partial w_w}$ and $\frac{\partial \pi_b}{\partial p_j}$ yields:

$$\frac{d\pi_b}{dw_w} = D_w + \sum_{j \in A \setminus b}\left[(p_b - c_b)\frac{\partial D_b}{\partial p_j} + (w_w - c_w)\frac{\partial D_w}{\partial p_j}\right]\frac{\partial p_j}{\partial w_w} = 0. \tag{3.7}$$

219. An increase in the wholesale price w_w leads to an increase in wholesale margins, which increases profits. This also leads to an increase in the entrant's retail price, which decreases the entrant's demand and thus wholesale revenues. The increase in the entrant's retail price also implies a positive effect, since some consumers switch to b's product. Finally, the increase in the wholesale price yields additional positive effects, since the increase in the other incumbents' prices positively affects both b's demand and the entrant's demand.

220. To obtain retail and wholesale's margins, we first need to compute $\frac{\partial p_j}{\partial w_w}$, the derivatives of all retail prices with respect to the wholesale price. To do so, we differentiate (5) and (6) with respect to the wholesale price w_w. This yields the two following conditions:

$$\underbrace{\sum_{j \in A}\left[\frac{\partial D_i}{\partial p_j} + (p_i - c_i)\frac{\partial^2 D_i}{\partial p_i \partial p_j} + I_{i=b}(w_w - c_w)\frac{\partial^2 D_w}{\partial p_i \partial p_j} + I_{j=i}\frac{\partial D_i}{\partial p_j}\right]}_{g_1(i,j)}$$

$$\frac{\partial p_j}{\partial w_w} + \underbrace{I_{i=b}\frac{\partial D_w}{\partial p_i}}_{h_1(i,w)} = 0, \tag{3.8}$$

$$\underbrace{\sum_{j \in A}\left[\frac{\partial D_w}{\partial p_j} + (p_w - w_w)\frac{\partial^2 D_w}{\partial p_w \partial p_j} + I_{j=w}\frac{\partial D_w}{\partial p_j}\right]}_{g_2(w,j)}\frac{\partial p_j}{\partial w_w} - \underbrace{\frac{\partial D_i}{\partial p_w}}_{h_2(w,w)} = 0. \tag{3.9}$$

221. We define G_1 as the matrix with element $g_1(i, j)$, G_2 the vector with element $g_2(w, j)$, and H_1 the vector with element $h_1(i, w)$. Stacking the matrix G_1 with the vector G_2, we obtain the matrix $G = \begin{bmatrix} G_1 \\ G_2 \end{bmatrix}$. Similarly, we define the vector $H = \begin{bmatrix} -H_1 \\ h_2(w, w) \end{bmatrix}$, by stacking the vector H_1 with the term $h_2(w, w)$. Letting Δ_p denote the vector with element $\frac{\partial p_j}{\partial w_w}$, we have:

$$\Delta_p = G^{-1}H.^{13} \tag{3.10}$$

222. To obtain retail and wholesale margins, we start by solving for the wholesale price using (6). We then plug the wholesale price in (5) and (7). Furthermore, we use (10) to substitute for Δ_p in (7). The retail and wholesale's margins are finally obtained by jointly solving (5) and (7).

3.4 Estimation and counterfactual analysis

223. ***Estimation.*** Building on the utility specified in Subsection 3.1, the demand in terms of market shares for each product can be expressed as follows:

$$\ln\left(\frac{s_{jt}}{s_{0t}}\right) = \mu_0 + \beta x_{jt} + \alpha p_{jt} + \sigma \ln(s_{j|gt}) + \xi_{jt}, \tag{3.11}$$

where s_{jt} is the market share of plan j in period t; $s_{j|gt}$ is the market share of plan j within nest g in period t; and s_{0t} is the market share of the outside option

13 To derive Δ_p from (8) and (9), we need to compute the first and second derivatives of market shares with respect to retail prices. We provide the formulas for the nested logit model in Appendix.

(whose associated utility is normalized to zero). A market is defined at the month level in our setting, and we define the total size of each market as the total number of consumers purchasing mobile services, including both postpaid and prepaid services. The outside option is thus given by the number of consumers purchasing prepaid plans.

224. To account for the endogeneity problem raised by the simultaneous relationship between prices, market shares and unobserved quality, we rely on instrumental variables. We use the sum and average of competing characteristics (call and data allowances) as instruments for the price. This set of instruments follows Berry, Levinsohn and Pakes (1995) as well as Verboven (1996) and represents isolation in the product space. Results are robust to different combinations of the instruments and the introduction of other instruments.[14]

225. Demand estimates are reported in Table 3. The first column shows regression results for a standard IV logit model, while the two other regressions show nested logit model results with two different specifications for nests.

	(1) Logit	(2) Nested Logit (1)	(3) Nested Logit (2)
Price	-0.131^{***} (0.043)	-0.048^{***} (0.008)	-0.055^{***} (0.010)
Data allowance (GB)	0.009^{***} (0.001)	0.002^{***} (0.000)	0.002^{***} (0.000)
Call allowance (100min)	0.116^{***} (0.020)	0.029^{***} (0.005)	0.035^{***} (0.006)
Entel	2.042^{***} (0.227)	0.392^{***} (0.091)	0.501^{***} (0.103)
Movistar	1.784^{***} (0.149)	0.275^{***} (0.085)	0.239^{**} (0.104)
Claro	0.987^{***} (0.115)	0.178^{***} (0.045)	0.092 (0.059)
Nest (σ)		0.881^{***} (0.051)	0.831^{***} (0.057)
Constant	-5.426^{***} (0.604)	-0.546 (0.346)	-1.319^{***} (0.373)
Year FE	Yes	Yes	Yes
Obs.	3554	3554	3554
R^2	0.41	0.98	0.97

Standard errors in parentheses
$^{*}p < 0.1$, $^{**}p < 0.05$, $^{***}p < 0.01$

Table 3.3: Demand estimates.

14 In particular, we used the sum and average characteristics of products within the same nest. We also used the square of data and call allowances.

226. ***Results.*** As expected, the average price has a significant negative impact on market shares. Our implied average price elasticity is 6.4, similar to other findings in the telecommunication literature.[15] Data and call allowances are found to have a positive and significant impact on market shares. Call allowances seem to have a larger impact than data allowances. This is probably due to the fact that the variation of observed data allowances in the data (0.1 to 420 GB) is very large compared to call allowances (55 to 3000min). From 2018 onwards, most plans exhibit the same call allowances and data allowance becomes the main variable for competition. Our estimates also indicate that some brands are more valued than others, Entel being the most valued one, followed by Movistar, Claro and WOM.

227. As mentioned above, we estimate two different nesting structure. In regression (2), we consider that all postpaid services belong to one nest, while prepaid services represent the other nest (the outside option). This is the same segmentation than the one used in Cojoc et al. (2020). Intuitively, this specification assumes that consumers choose first whether they want to purchase prepaid or postpaid services, and then in a second stage they choose which operator to buy from. The within-group correlation parameter (σ) is very large, suggesting strong correlated preferences for postpaid services. In regression (3), we test another specification of nests, considering that Entel and WOM belong to one nest and Movistar and Claro to another nest. This nesting structure may be justified by the fact that WOM relied on Entel's network upon entry, and so consumers may associate WOM's quality to the one of Entel.[16] Again, the within-group correlation parameter is very large. It is difficult to determine which nesting structure is the most appropriate and realistic. One of the main drawback of the nested logit model is that nests are arbitrarily defined, and the way nests are defined entails important differences in estimated substitution patterns and counterfactual analysis, when combined with the supply side. In what follows, we use the nests and estimates from regression (3) to conduct our counterfactual analysis. The main reason is that two products that belong to the same nests exhibit higher cross-price elasticities, which leads to strong reactions following a change in the market structure. Given the important price response of Entel to WOM's switch in access provider, this nesting structure seems to be the most appropriate to predict counterfactual outcomes.[17]

---

15 See Bourreau et al., (2021), Huang (2008), Kim et al., (2010), and Grzybowski and Pereira (2007) for related studies.

16 We also estimated another nesting structure, taking Claro and WOM as part of the same nest, and Entel and Movistar as part of another nest. WOM and Claro typically propose the cheapest plans in the market and tend to target young users, while Entel and Movistar are the most (longest) established firms in the market.

17 The random coefficient logit model does not put such restrictions on substitutions patterns between firms. We are currently working on the implementation of this model.

228. ***Counterfactual analysis.*** Figure 2 below shows the evolution of Entel's average price over time. The average price of Entel slightly increases after entry in June 2015 and remained quite high until the beginning of 2017. However, the average price exhibits a clear drop around the first months of 2017. This corresponds to the emergence of tensions between WOM and Entel over the renegotiation of the roaming contract. The formal change in access supplier is represented by the dashed vertical line. These observations seem consistent with our prediction that providing access to the entrant limits incentives to decrease prices. The change in access provider from WOM deprived Entel from access revenues, which made downstream revenues more important for Entel. We combine the estimates from our demand model with the supply model to study Entel's counterfactual price. In our observation period (October 2017-June 2022), Movistar is the roaming partner of WOM. We estimate the prices that Entel would have charged if it had been providing access to WOM during this period, as it did a few months before. The predicted price appears in Figure 2. Although the fact that Entel's average price would have been higher than the one observed is mainly due to the theoretical supply model, the magnitude of the price increase stems from our demand estimates. Our predicted price increase matches reasonably well Entel's average price before the switch of access provider. Our empirical model thus helps rationalize the price drop that followed WOM's switch in access provider. We take this as further empirical evidence that in vertically integrated markets, providing an input to a downstream competitor reduces the incentives of the input provider to decrease prices.

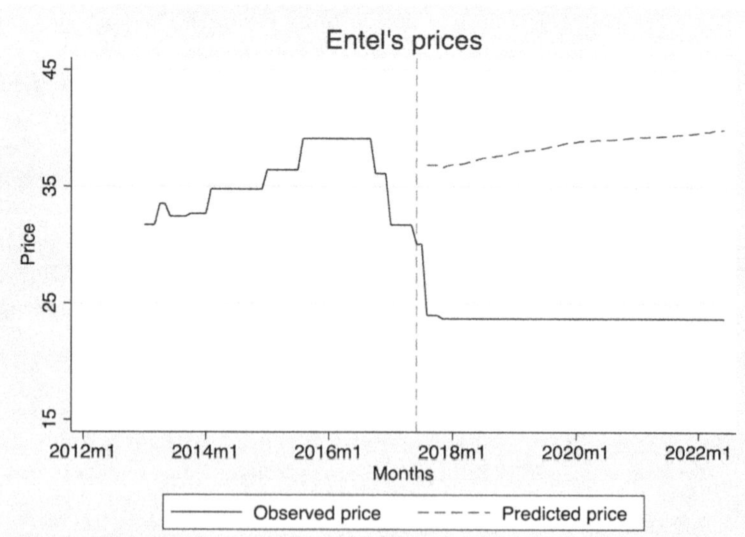

Figure 3.2: Counterfactual prices

3.5 Conclusion

229. We have analyzed the impact of entry in the market for mobile telecommunications in Chile. More precisely, we have studied how network access provision affects a firm's pricing strategy in the downstream market. We use detailed information on plans' characteristics over a large time period (2013-2022) to estimate the impact of entry on firms' prices and market shares. We also use unique information on plan-level market shares for the four main operators in the market over the period 2017-2022 to estimate a differentiated product demand model. We combine these estimates with an oligopoly model of wholesale and retail price competition to rationalize a sudden decrease in retail prices following a change in access provider.

230. Our findings show that entry did not affect firms' pricing strategies in the same way. The operator that provided access to the entrant did not decrease prices in the months that followed entry, in contrast to the two other incumbents in the market. This resulted in an asymmetric cannibalization of market shares by the entrant. While the access provider rapidly lost many costumers after entry, the two other incumbents only experienced moderate decrease in their market shares. These empirical results support our prediction that the access provider had less incentives than other incumbents to decrease prices upon entry. We also show that these incentives were substantially altered when the entrant switched to another incumbent for network access.

231. Our results provide support for the use of structural empirical models to inform how changes in market structure affect firms' prices. Our demand estimates and counterfactual analysis yields realistic predictions, in line with prices observed before the change in access provider. The use and development of such methods at competition authorities and regulation agencies is of primary importance.

References

Angrist, J. D., & Pischke, J. S. (2010). The credibility revolution in empirical economics: How better research design is taking the con out of econometrics. *Journal of economic perspectives*, 24(2), 3-30.

Berto Villas-Boas, S. (2007). Vertical relationships between manufacturers and retailers: Inference with limited data. *The Review of Economic Studies*, 74(2), 625-652.

Björnerstedt, J., & Verboven, F. (2016). Does merger simulation work? Evidence from the Swedish analgesics market. *American Economic Journal: Applied Economics*, 8(3), 125-64.

Bonnet, C., & Dubois, P. (2010). Inference on vertical contracts between manufacturers and retailers allowing for nonlinear pricing and resale price maintenance. *The RAND Journal of Economics*, 41(1), 139-164.

Bourreau, M., Hombert, J., Pouyet, J., & Schutz, N. (2011). Upstream competition between vertically integrated firms. *The Journal of Industrial Economics*, 59(4), 677-713.

Bourreau, M., Sun, Y., & Verboven, F. (2021). Market entry, fighting brands, and tacit collusion: Evidence from the French mobile telecommunications market. *American Economic Review*, 111(11), 3459-99.

Cojoc, A., Ivaldi, M., Maier-Rigaud, F. P., & März, O. (2020). Horizontal cooperation on investment: Evidence from mobile network sharing.

Goolsbee, A., & Syverson, C. (2008). How do incumbents respond to the threat of entry? Evidence from the major airlines. *The Quarterly journal of economics*, 123(4), 1611-1633.

Hart, O., Tirole, J., Carlton, D. W., & Williamson, O. E. (1990). Vertical integration and market foreclosure. *Brookings papers on economic activity. Microeconomics*, 1990, 205-286.

Hastings, J. S. (2004). Vertical relationships and competition in retail gasoline markets: Empirical evidence from contract changes in Southern California. *American Economic Review*, 94(1), 317-328.

Luco, F., & Marshall, G. (2020). The competitive impact of vertical integration by multi-product firms. *American Economic Review*, 110(7), 2041-64.

Miller, N. H., & Weinberg, M. C. (2017). Understanding the price effects of the Miller-Coors joint venture. *Econometrica*, 85(6), 1763-1791.

Nevo, A., Whinston, M. D. (2010). Taking the dogma out of econometrics: Structural modeling and credible inference. *Journal of Economic Perspectives*, 24(2), 69-82.

Nicolle, A., Grzybowski, L., & Zulehner, C. (2018). Impact Of Competition, Investment, And Regulation On Prices Of Mobile Services: Evidence From France. *Economic Inquiry*, 56(2), 1322-1345.

Ordover, J., & Shaffer, G. (2007). Wholesale access in multi-firm markets: When is it profitable to supply a competitor?. *International Journal of Industrial Organization*, 25(5), 1026-1045.

Ordover, J. A., Saloner, G., & Salop, S. C. (1990). Equilibrium vertical foreclosure. *The American Economic Review*, 127-142.

Salinger, M. A. (1988). Vertical mergers and market foreclosure. *The Quarterly Journal of Economics*, 103(2), 345-356.

Seim, K., & Viard, V. B. (2011). The effect of market structure on cellular technology adoption and pricing. *American economic journal: Microeconomics*, 3(2), 221-51.

Train, K. E. (2009). Discrete choice methods with simulation. Cambridge university press.

APPENDICES

A.1 Hedonic price regressions

232. To gain further insights about the evolution of prices and assess the robustness of the results of section 2, we conduct hedonic price regressions. Hedonic price regressions are widely used in the telecommunication sector. In particular, we follow the approach of Nicolle et al., 2018. It allows to evaluate the evolution of quality-adjusted prices over time. We estimate the following regression:

$$p_{jt} = \alpha + \beta X_{jt} + \eta_t + \tau_o + \epsilon_{jt}, \quad \text{(A.12)}$$

where p_{jt} is the price of plan j in month t, X_{jt} is a vector of plan characteristics; the two subsequent terms represent month and operator fixed effects and ϵ_{jt} is the error term. The coefficients η_t represent the evolution of quality-adjusted prices over time. We estimate this regression over the whole set of mobile tariffs available and separately for each incumbent operator. The results are reported in Table 4 below. All variables are highly significant and have the expected sign. Higher data and call allowances are associated to higher prices, and the three incumbents firms charge higher prices than the entrant. In Figure 3, we draw the evolution of month coefficients, which shows how quality-adjusted prices have evolved through time. While the two incumbents Movistar and Claro decreased their prices upon entry, Entel's prices seem to have remained relatively constant until the change in access provider, where we observe a clear cut in price. We take this as further evidence of the weaker incentives of the access provider to reduce its price after entry.

	(1) **All firms**	(2) **Entel**	(3) **Movistar**	(4) **Claro**
Data Allowance	0.371*** (0.033)	0.320*** (0.073)	0.661*** (0.046)	0.667*** (0.072)
Call Allowance (100-400)	10.622*** (0.463)	9.808*** (0.644)	10.847*** (0.573)	13.421*** (1.058)

	(1) All firms	(2) Entel	(3) Movistar	(4) Claro
Call Allowance (400-800)	19.286*** (0.571)	19.294*** (0.914)	19.674*** (0.796)	24.550*** (1.262)
Call Allowance (800-3200)	39.093*** (0.738)	44.789*** (1.142)	42.758*** (1.041)	43.843*** (1.444)
Call Allowance (unlimited)	33.902*** (1.121)	35.953*** (1.575)	27.349*** (2.140)	36.999*** (2.810)
Entel	8.989*** (0.829)			
Movistar	6.651*** (0.860)			
Claro	5.188*** (0.841)			
Month FE	Yes	Yes	Yes	Yes
Obs.	2229	616	700	730
R^2	0.78	0.80	0.81	0.84

Standard errors in parentheses

* $p < 0.1$, ** $p < 0.05$, *** $p < 0.01$

Table A.4: Hedonic regressions

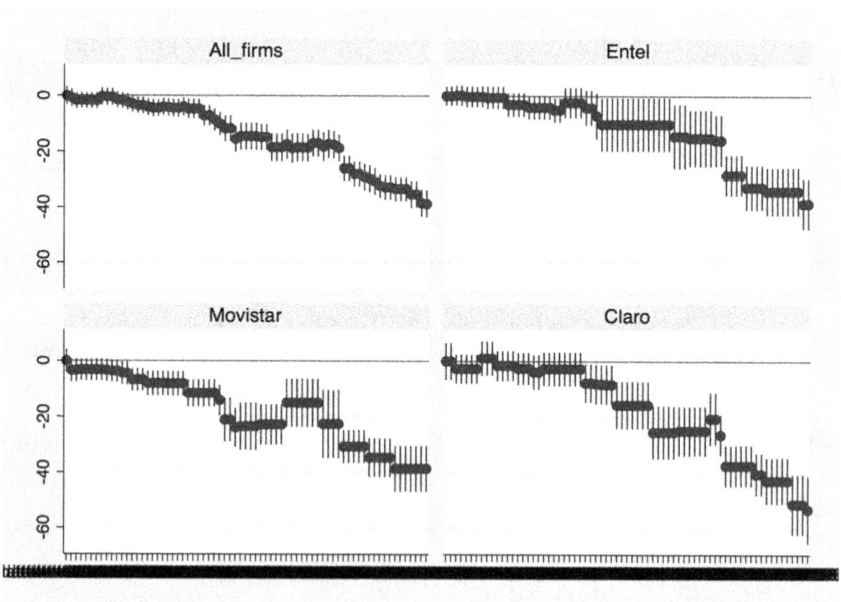

Figure A.3: Evolution of quality adjusted prices.

A.2 Computation of demand derivatives with respect to price

233. First, let us state the expression for the choice probability in the nested logit model: $s_j = s_{j|g}\, s_{g.}$ The probability of choosing product j is simply the product of the probability to choose a product in nest g and the probability of choosing product i given that nest g has been chosen (see Train, 2009, p.82). We have:

$$s_j = \frac{e^{\frac{\alpha p_j + \sum_x \beta_n x_{nj} + \xi_j}{1-\sigma_g}}}{\sum_{j\in F_g} e^{\frac{\alpha p_j + \sum_x \beta_n x_{nj} + \xi_j}{1-\sigma_g}}} \frac{e^{(1-\sigma_g)\ln\left(\sum_{j\in F_g} e^{\frac{\alpha p_j + \Sigma_x \beta_n x_{nj} + \xi_j}{1-\sigma_g}}\right)}}{\sum_{g=1}^{G} e^{(1-\sigma_g)\ln\left(\sum_{j\in F_g} e^{\frac{\alpha p_j + \Sigma_x \beta_n x_{nj} + \xi_j}{1-\sigma_g}}\right)}}, \tag{A.13}$$

where the first term (fraction) represents the conditional probability of choosing product i given that a product in nest g is chosen, and the second term is the probability of choosing a product in nest g. The interest of this decomposition is that it allows to express the nested logit probability as the product of two simple logit probabilities.

234. We now derive first and second price derivatives of market shares with respect to price. The first derivative of a firm's market shares with respect to price is given by:

$$\frac{\partial s_j}{\partial p_k} = \begin{cases} \alpha s_j\left(\frac{1}{1-\sigma} - \frac{\sigma}{1-\sigma} s_{j|g} - s_j\right) & \text{if} \quad k = j \\ -\alpha s_k\left(\frac{1}{1-\sigma} s_{j|g} + s_j\right) & \text{if} \quad k \neq j \quad \text{and} \quad k, j \quad \text{in the same nest} \\ -\alpha s_j s_k & \text{if} \quad k \neq j \quad \text{and} \quad k, j \quad \text{in the same nests.} \end{cases}$$

235. An equivalent (but more handy) formula for the second equation (cross derivative for products in the same nest) is given by: $\frac{\partial s_j}{\partial p_k} = \alpha s_k s_j \left(1 + \frac{\sigma}{1-\sigma}\frac{1}{s_g}\right)$.

236. To obtain the second derivatives of shares with respect to prices, one first needs to compute the derivatives of conditional share:

$$\frac{\partial s_{j|g}}{\partial p_k} = \begin{cases} \frac{\alpha}{1-\sigma} s_{j|g}(1 - s_{j|g}) & \text{if} \quad k = j \\ -\frac{\alpha}{1-\sigma} s_{j|g} s_{k|g} & \text{if} \quad k \neq j \quad \text{and} \quad k, j \quad \text{in the same nest} \\ 0 & \text{if} \quad k \neq j \quad \text{and} \quad k, j \quad \text{in the same nests.} \end{cases}$$

237. For completeness, we also compute the derivatives of group shares with respect to prices:

$$\frac{\partial s_g}{\partial p_k} = \begin{cases} \alpha s_k\left(1 - s_g\right) & \text{if } k \text{ is in nest } g \\ -\alpha s_g s_k & \text{if } k \text{ is in nest } g \end{cases}$$

238. We now compute the second derivatives of shares with respect to prices $\left(\frac{\partial^2 s_j}{\partial p_k \partial p_l}\right)$. There are several cases to consider.

239. **Own-own derivative.** The second derivative of firm *j*'s share with respect to its own price is given by:

$$\frac{\partial^2 s_j}{\partial^2 p_j} = \alpha^2 s_j\left[\frac{1}{1-\sigma} - \frac{\sigma s_{j|g}}{1-\sigma} - s_j\right]\left[\frac{1}{1-\sigma} - \frac{\sigma s_{j|g}}{1-\sigma} - 2s_j\right]$$
$$- \alpha^2 \frac{\sigma}{(1-\sigma)^2} s_j s_{j|g}(1 - s_{j|g}).$$

240. **Own-cross derivative.** The second derivative of firm *j*'s share with respect to its own price and that of another product *k*, *k* and *j* belonging to different nests, is given by:

$$\frac{\partial^2 s_j}{\partial p_j \partial p_k} = -\alpha^2 s_j s_k\left(\frac{1}{1-\sigma} - \frac{\sigma}{1-\sigma} s_{j|g} - s_j\right) + \alpha^2 s_j^2 s_k.$$

241. **Own-cross derivative.** The second derivative of firm *j*'s share with respect to its own price and that of another product *k*, *k* and *j* belonging to the same nest, is given by:

$$\frac{\partial^2 s_j}{\partial p_j \partial p_k} = \alpha^2\left[-s_k\left(\frac{\sigma}{1-\sigma} s_{j|g} + s_j\right)\left(\frac{1}{1-\sigma} - \frac{\sigma}{1-\sigma} s_{j|g} - s_j\right)\right.$$
$$\left. + s_j\left(\frac{\sigma}{\left(1-\sigma\right)^2} s_{j|g} s_{k|g} + s_k\left(\frac{\sigma}{1-\sigma} s_{j|g} + s_j\right)\right)\right]$$

242. **Cross-cross derivative.** The second derivative of firm *j*'s share with respect to the price of product *k* and *l*, with *j*, *k* and *l* in three different nests (note that this scenario does not occur in our current set-up, since we have only two nests), is given by:

$$\frac{\partial^2 s_j}{\partial p_k \partial p_l} = 2\alpha^2 s_j s_k s_l.$$

243. **Cross-cross derivative.** The second derivative of firm *j*'s share with respect to the price of product *k* and *l*, with *k* and *l* in the same nest but different than that of *j*, is given by:

$$\frac{\partial^2 s_j}{\partial p_k \partial p_l} = \alpha^2 \left[s_j s_k s_l + s_j s_l \left(\frac{\sigma}{1-\sigma} s_{k|g} + s_k \right) \right].$$

244. **Cross-cross derivative.** The second derivative of firm *j*'s share with respect to the price of product *k* and *l*, with *k*, *l* and *j* all belonging to the same nest (note that this scenario does not occur in our current set-up, since we have four single-product firms, and two firms in each nest), is given by:

$$\frac{\partial^2 s_j}{\partial p_k \partial p_l} = \alpha^2 \left[2 s_k s_j s_l \left(1 + \frac{\sigma}{1-\sigma} \frac{1}{s_g} \right) + s_k s_j s_l \left(\frac{\sigma}{1-\sigma} \frac{1-s_g}{s_g^2} \right) \right].$$

245. **Cross-cross derivative.** The second derivative of firm *j*'s share with respect to the price of product *k* and *l*, with *j* and *k* in the same nest, and *l* belonging to another nest, is given by:

$$\frac{\partial^2 s_j}{\partial p_k \partial p_l} = \alpha^2 \left[s_j s_k s_l \left(2 + \frac{\sigma}{1-\sigma} \frac{1}{s_g} \right) \right].$$

246. **Cross-cross derivative.** The second derivative of firm *j*'s share with respect to the price of product *k*, with *j* and *k* in the same nest, is given by:

$$\frac{\partial^2 s_j}{\partial p_k} = \alpha^2 \left[-s_k \frac{\sigma}{1 \ \sigma} \left(1 - \sigma s_{k|g} - (1-\sigma) s_k \right) \left(s_j + \frac{\sigma}{1-\sigma} s_{j|g} \right) \right.$$
$$\left. + s_k \left(\frac{\sigma}{1-\sigma} \frac{\sigma}{1-\sigma} s_{j|g} s_{k|g} + s_k \left(\frac{\sigma}{1-\sigma} s_{j|g} + s_j \right) \right) \right].$$

247. **Cross-cross derivative.** The second derivative of firm *j*'s share with respect to the price of product *k*, with *j* and *k* not in the same nest, is given by:

$$\frac{\partial^2 s_j}{\partial^2 p_k} = \alpha^2 s_j s_k \left[s_k - \frac{1}{1-\sigma} \left(1 - \sigma s_{k|g} - (1-\sigma) s_k \right) \right].$$

CONCLUSION

248. Our modern societies are built on the idea that overall economic well-being is best achieved by leaving individuals pursue their own interests, with minimum intervention of public authorities. This philosophy, first developed by famous political economist Adam Smith in his 1776 book *The Wealth of Nations*, is at the core of market economies. This is illustrated by his celebrated quote: "*Every individual...neither intends to promote the public interest, nor knows how much he is promoting it... He intends only his own gain, and he is in this, as in many other cases, led by an invisible hand to promote an end which was no part of it. By pursuing his own interest he frequently promotes that of the society more effectually than when he really intends to promote it.*"

249. While the main precepts of Adam Smith are still very relevant, it has become clear that markets sometimes fail and that market power, a prominent cause of market failure, must be kept in check. As highlighted by Jean Tirole, one of the world's most influential economist in the analysis of market power: "*The theory of industrial organization has proved a very useful tool to think about one of the major challenges of our economies. It has fashioned antitrust and regulation.*"[1] In his 2014 Nobel Prize lecture, he also points out: "*Industrial organization has gone a long way, but much work remains to be done.*"

250. In this thesis, we attempted to make a modest contribution to the literature on industrial organization. We first investigated some of the challenges raised by the recent development of digital economics. Digital markets are evolving rapidly and thus, public authorities need to understand how these markets work to evaluate the merit of various policies.

251. In Chapter 1 of this thesis, we studied how firms' incentives to produce differentiated products in multisided media markets differ from more traditional markets. We have shown that firms operating in media markets devote significant attention to the composition of their demand (i.e., the share of exclusive and multihoming consumers), while firms operating in more

1 Jean Tirole, 2014 Nobel Prize lecture, reprinted in Tirole (2015).

traditional markets essentially focus on total demand. Indeed, if advertisers are not willing to pay the same price for a first and a second impression, demand composition matters for firms' profits (i.e., multihoming consumers tend to be less valuable than exclusive ones). We show that if differentiation leads to an increase in the number of (less-valuable) multihoming consumers, firms operating in media markets will have limited incentives to differentiate. Conversely, since all consumers generate the same value in more traditional market, firms are mainly interested in the effect of differentiation on the total size of demand. In particular, if differentiation leads to market expansion, firms have incentives to differentiate.

252. Our work contributes to the policy debate around mergers in multisided markets, and more particularly to the question of whether such mergers should be assessed differently than in standard markets. We note that the two recent regulations voted in the EU, the DMA and the DSA, remain surprisingly silent on mergers. We show that mergers can restore firms' incentives to differentiate in media markets. This positive effect should be accounted for when analyzing mergers in media markets. However, we also show that this positive effect on product variety comes at the cost of higher prices for advertisers. An appropriate competition policy must thus evaluate the likely magnitude of these two effects to decide whether to clear the merger or not.

253. In Chapter 2 of this thesis, we explored the informational issues surrounding digital platforms. Indeed, while many digital platforms provide rich information to consumers and help them make better decisions, such environments are often subject to biased recommendations.[2] Accordingly, we have studied the merit of stricter disclosure rules, or minimum message length policy, in environments that involve an informed adviser and an uninformed decision maker. We have studied the circumstances in which such rules can improve individuals' decisions. We have shown that the benefit of a stricter disclosure rule hinges on the (ex-ante) alignment of the parties' interests and the quality of the adviser's information. In particular, the effect of the policy is less likely to be positive when the expertise of the adviser is high. We have also shown that the adviser doesn't have incentives to acquire more precise information than what is necessary to manipulate the decision maker, and that a stricter policy can improve these incentives.

254. Our analysis focused on a single adviser-single decision maker setting. Our results deserve to be discussed in richer environments. In particular, one may wonder how the incentives of the adviser for information acquisition are affected when he faces several decision makers with different levels of ex-ante confidence in the action considered, as is typically the case with recommendation platforms.

2 As we discuss in the paper, such issues extend beyond the environment of platforms.

255. In Chapter 3, we studied another central issue in industrial organization: the effect of new entry on firms' prices. More specifically, we explored the strategic relations between integrated incumbents and a new entrant in the Chilean mobile telecommunications market. In such integrated markets, incentives to decrease prices are more subtle than in more standard markets. We have shown that the access provider had less incentives to decrease its retail prices following entry. Accordingly, the access provider's market share was more affected than the other incumbents in the market. We have used an empirical oligopoly model to rationalize a sudden decrease in retail prices that resulted from a change in access supplier. Our counterfactual estimates predicted reasonably well the observed price drop.

256. Structural models of demand and supply represent the only way to predict counterfactual outcomes, a key aspect in the assessment of any decision by a public authority. Nevertheless, these models remain relatively underused by competition authorities. Economic research is flourishing is this area, and these methods are becoming increasingly reliable. More dialogue is needed between researchers and public authorities the implement these methods more regularly in the near future.

References

Smith, Adam (1776). The wealth of nations.

Tirole, Jean (2015). Market failures and public policy. American Economic Review, 105(6), 1665-82.

Concurrences
Competition Laws Review

Concurrences Review

Concurrences is a print and online quarterly peer reviewed journal dedicated to EU and national competitions laws. It has been launched in 2004 as the flagship of the Institute of Competition Law in order to provide a forum for academics, practitioners and enforcers. Concurrences' influence and expertise has garnered contributions or interviews with such figures as Christine Lagarde, Bill Kovacic, Emmanuel Macron, Antonin Scalia and Magrethe Vestager.

Contents

More than 15,500 articles, print and/or online. Quarterly issues provide current coverage with contributions from the EU or national or foreign countries thanks to more than 2,500 authors in Europe and abroad.

Format

In order to balance academic contributions with opinions or legal practice notes, Concurrences provides its insight and analysis in a number of formats:

- Forewords: Opinions by leading academics or enforcers
- Interviews: Interviews of antitrust experts
- On-Topics: 4 to 6 short papers on hot issues
- Law & Economics: Short papers written by economists for a legal audience
- Articles: Long academic papers
- Case Summaries: Case commentary on EU and French case law
- Legal Practice: Short papers for in-house counsels
- International: Medium size papers on international policies
- Books Review: Summaries of recent antitrust books
- Articles Review: Summaries of leading articles published in 45 antitrust journals

Boards

The Scientific Committee is headed by Laurence Idot, Professor at Panthéon Assas University. The International Committee is headed by Frederic Jenny, OECD Competition Comitteee Chairman. Boards members include Douglas Ginsburg, Benoît Cœuré, Howard Shelanski, Richard Whish, Wouter Wils, Joshua Wright, etc.

Online version

Concurrences website provides all articles published since its inception, in addition to selected articles published online only in the electronic supplement.

Write for Concurrences

Concurrences welcome spontaneous contributions. Except in rare circumstances, the journal accepts only unpublished articles, whatever the form and nature of the contribution. The Editorial Board checks the form of the proposals, and then submits these to the Scientific Committee. Selection of the papers is conditional to a peer review by at least two members of the Committee. Within a month, the Committee assesses whether the draft article can be published and notifies the author.